# Daily Devotional

Luke Harding

Copyright © 2024
LUKE HARDING

All rights reserved. No portion of this book may be reproduced, copied, distributed or adapted in any way, except for certain activities permitted by applicable copyright laws, such as brief quotations in the context of a review or article. For permission to publish, distribute or otherwise reproduce this work, please contact the author.

Scriptures taken from the Holy Bible, New International Version®, NIV®. Copyright © 1973, 1978, 1984, 2011 by Biblica, Inc.™ Used by permission of Zondervan. All rights reserved worldwide. www.zondervan.com The "NIV" and "New International Version" are trademarks registered in the United States Patent and Trademark Office by Biblica, Inc.™

Printed in the United Kingdom
First Printing Edition, 2024
ISBN 9798303270695

## *Forward*

For as long as I can remember, I have always used Christian devotionals alongside my morning Bible readings and prayers. They have been a great inspiration and supplement to the Word and have provided encouragement and motivation for the day ahead.

After years of making notes and putting together my own thoughts on the truths of scripture, I decided to compile my own devotional to equip others in their Christian walk and to help them keep going in their pursuit of Jesus.

Whether you read these short messages in the morning or the evening, I pray that they will be a reminder that you are an overcomer and can do all things through Christ who strengthens you and that you can run your race well to the end, which you will in Jesus' name, amen.

# Daily Devotional

# January 1

*But Caleb quieted the people before Moses and said, "Let us go up at once and occupy it, for we are well able to overcome it."*
Numbers 13:30

God's Promised Land lies before us this year and we can either say "yes Lord I'm ready to go in and take the giants and possess the land" or shrink back in fear. The latter option shouldn't even be an option for us, for God will not be pleased with us if we do. Instead let's go forward in faith believing that all things are possible for "we do not belong to those who shrink back and are destroyed, but to those who have faith and are saved" (Hebrews 10:39).

# January 2

*Tell the righteous that it shall be well with them, for they shall eat the fruit of their deeds.* Isaiah 3:10

When the spies went up to Canaan, only two came back with a positive report. They all saw the land, the giants and the abundance, but only two had faith that God would give it over to them. Without faith we cannot please God or enter into His promises, but with faith we can be sure of a good reward as we hold on to God's word continually. Hebrews 11:6 confirms this in saying "without faith it is impossible to please him, for whoever would draw near to God must believe that he exists and that he rewards those who seek him." Make a decision to seek the Lord today and trust Him with your life, family and future so that you can also boldly declare, "I have faith in God that it will happen just as he told me" (Acts 27:25).

## January 3

"Do not call conspiracy all that this people calls conspiracy, and do not fear what they fear, nor be in dread. But the LORD of hosts, him you shall honour as holy. Let him be your fear, and let him be your dread. Isaiah 8:12-13

There are many conspiracy theories in the world today and some do have some truth to them. People are also fearful about what could happen in these last days. As God's people though we are not given to fear and speculation. Instead, we stand on the Word of God that never changes and which promises peace and protection to those who walk uprightly before Him. Make the decision to be more mindful of what God is saying today than what the world is communicating and suggesting.

## January 4

...and the LORD spoke to Moses, saying, "Take the staff, and assemble the congregation, you and Aaron your brother, and tell the rock before their eyes to yield its water. So you shall bring water out of the rock for them and give drink to the congregation and their cattle." Numbers 20:7-8

On a previous occasion, Moses was told to strike a rock in order to get water from it for the people. This was a picture of Jesus going to the cross and being struck by God for our sins. From the cross now flows life and salvation for all who believe. When we put our faith in the redeeming work of Jesus, we enter a new walk of faith that is activated by our words so that we can speak into our situations by faith and expect it to change. What do you need to speak to today? Even if it looks like an immovable rock, we can tell this mountain to be removed and thrown into the sea.

# January 5

*So Moses made a bronze serpent and set it on a pole. And if a serpent bit anyone, he would look at the bronze serpent and live.*
Numbers 21:9

People are being bit by sin all the time and feeling the effects of its sting, but thank God we have a redeemer and a way of escape through Jesus Christ so that when we look to the cross and to His death and resurrection, we find forgiveness, healing, hope and life. It seems simple but we just have to look to Him and put our faith in Him in the same way the Israelites had to believe in the healing effect of looking to the bronze serpent on the pole in the wilderness.

# January 6

*"Therefore I tell you, whatever you ask for in prayer, believe that you have received it, and it will be yours. And when you stand praying, if you hold anything against anyone, forgive them, so that your Father in heaven may forgive you your sins."* Mark 11:24-25

Jesus gives us two big keys to answered prayer in this passage. The first is to have faith that it has been heard in heaven and will be released on earth and the second is to relinquish any resentment or unforgiveness that we might be carrying. Doubt will block the promises of God from being carried out and so too will the refusal to give up any offenses that others have caused us. Come to God with a clean heart and conscience today and believe that He is working on your behalf in response to your prayers. He always hears us when we pray.

## January 7

*But when they told him everything Joseph had said to them, and when he saw the carts Joseph had sent to carry him back, the spirit of their father Jacob revived. Genesis 45:27*

When Jacob heard that Joseph was still alive and ruling in Egypt, his spirit came alive and hope returned. Joseph is a type of Christ and in the same way when someone hears the good news of what Jesus has done for them at the cross and responds, their spirit comes alive and they are born again! There is no hope outside of Christ and His sacrificial death on the cross for no one else has risen from the grave to show us that we can free from sin, death and hell forevermore. Don't stop sharing with others what God has done for them so that they too can come alive to new life today.

## January 8

*...and they asked each other, "Who will roll the stone away from the entrance of the tomb?" But when they looked up, they saw that the stone, which was very large, had been rolled away. Mark 16:3-4*

I love this part of the resurrection story! The faithful female disciples were determined to anoint the body of Jesus according to custom but knew they would face a major challenge in trying to move the grave stone. When they arrived, they found that it had already been rolled away and all their questioning and worrying was for nothing. Not only that but they didn't need to anoint Jesus because He had risen from the dead! Remember this story the next time you are facing a seemingly insurmountable obstacle and believe that God can move the mountains in your way before you even reach them.

## January 9

*How can a young man keep his way pure? By living according to your word. I seek you with all my heart; do not let me stray from your commands. Psalm 119:99*

The word of God will keep us doing what is right while on the path that is right. We do not need social media, AI, Google or Siri to show us which way to go - we need a timely word from the Lord every day to guide us, keep us and empower us for service. How do we get this word? We read the Bible and study it daily and we sit with Jesus in His presence until we hear Him speak to us and He will if we are listening. The word of God is pure and will inwardly wash us clean as we consume it. We need it more than anything else today.

## January 10

*Therefore, say to the Israelites: 'I am the LORD, and I will bring you out from under the yoke of the Egyptians. I will free you from being slaves to them, and I will redeem you with an outstretched arm and with mighty acts of judgment. Exodus 6:6*

God promised freedom to the Israelites despite their harsh conditions and slavery and He has promised freedom to us through the death and resurrection of Jesus His Son. The power of the cross is able to break any yoke that we find ourselves under. We just need to apply the blood of Jesus to the chains that hold us and believe that we are already free because of His sacrifice. Do not be content to stay bound or in any kind of torment of the enemy - you and I were made to walk free and reign with Christ in His victorious resurrection power.

## January 11

> Their father Jacob said to them, "You have deprived me of my children. Joseph is no more and Simeon is no more, and now you want to take Benjamin. Everything is against me! Genesis 42:36

Have you ever felt like everything was against you like Jacob did? I'm sure we've been in that place more than once and it makes us question why. Is it because of something we've done or not done, or because of something from the past? We don't know why Jacob went through this trial with Joseph, but we do know that God was working behind the scenes for good and was using it all to deliver Israel and his family from famine and death. If you're feeling like the world is against you then ask the Holy Spirit to reveal what is going on and the reason for it. You may be on the brink of a major blessing and the enemy is trying to preempt it and prevent you from receiving it, so make the decision to keep praising and seeking the Lord until He turns it all around which He will.

## January 12

> You crown the year with your bounty, and your carts overflow with abundance. Psalm 65:11

This verse is especially popular at the start of a new year for it announces the goodness and provision of God for the land and its people. God is our provider and will supply all our needs according to His riches in glory in Christ Jesus. We do not need to look to people or our own strength, but to El Shaddai (God Almighty) and Jehovah Jireh (The Lord will provide) and trust Him to sustain and support us from the beginning to the end of the year.

## January 13

*And there were shepherds living out in the fields nearby, keeping watch over their flocks at night. An angel of the Lord appeared to them, and the glory of the Lord shone around them, and they were terrified. Luke 2:8*

This could be a prophetic picture of the church in the world today. For we are living in the night season before Jesus comes back and a new dawn appears and our role is to shepherd God's people in the meantime, which means to protect them, pray for them, encourage and equip them. We can do this as a full time pastor, as a parent, as a mentor or simply as a friend. All of us can watch out for another fellow believer in our lives and keep them in prayer before the Lord. Remember there is a crown and reward promised for those who are faithful in fulfilling this so let's be diligent and pray also for the spiritual shepherds who are watching over us.

## January 14

*While Israel lived in Shittim, the people began to whore with the daughters of Moab. Numbers 25:1*

Barak, the king of Moab, had tried to curse Israel through Balaam but it resulted in the nation receiving a blessing instead. God supernaturally delivered them, for "an undeserved curse does not come to rest" (Proverbs 26:2). The enemy then tried to destroy them through seduction and many of the men of Israel were led into sexual immorality and worship of Baal of Peor through the Midianite women. If the devil cannot get us one way, he will often try another strategy which is why we must always be on guard against his wiles and deception. Keep your eyes on Jesus today.

## January 15

*But now the Lord says: "Within three years, as a servant bound by contract would count them, Moab's splendor and all her many people will be despised, and her survivors will be very few and feeble." Isaiah 16:14*

There are certain time periods that are significant in the bible. Among them is three years. We know that Jesus ministered for just over three years before going to the cross and that He was thirty-three years old when he ascended back to heaven. Daniel and his friends were trained for three years before entering the service of the king of Babylon. Jesus told the parable of a landowner who had been looking for fruit for three years. As pastors, we have found that people often come to the Lord after three years of praying for them. Be encouraged that things can change for good after three years, especially if we stay in prayer and faith in God.

## January 16

*And after you have suffered a little while, the God of all grace, who has called you to his eternal glory in Christ, will himself restore, confirm, strengthen, and establish you. 1 Peter 5:10*

In this chapter, Peter warned the elders of the church to shepherd and lead the people righteously since they would stand before God and be accountable to the Chief Shepherd in eternity. He was also warning them of the coming judgement in the church that neither the leaders nor the people would escape from, but he ends on a high note of hope that after suffering there would be glory, restoration and establishment again. This is a powerful promise and reminder for us today as we go through various trials and tests that serve to refine our faith.

## January 17

*The seven years of abundance in Egypt came to an end, and the seven years of famine began, just as Joseph had said. There was famine in all the other lands, but in the whole land of Egypt there was food. Genesis 41:53-54*

When Israel turned away from God, He would often use disease, famine or war to bring them back to Himself. The same judgments will be used in the tribulation period as a result of people's rebellion and rejection of God's mercy and salvation. There is no doubt that famine and shortages will come and they are already here in some parts of the world, but the good news is that even in the midst of such conditions, God has continued to provide for those who love Him. In fact, Psalm 37:19 gives an even greater promise for the righteous when it says, "In times of disaster they will not wither; in days of famine they will enjoy plenty." Isaac proved this when he "planted crops in that land and the same year reaped a hundredfold, because the LORD blessed him" (Genesis 26:12).

## January 18

*...the Lord knows how to rescue the godly from trials. 2 Peter 2:4*

God doesn't keep us from trials and difficulties but rather delivers us out of them when we cry out to Him. He also uses them to refine us and make us more like Jesus. Peter tells us that we can be confident in this knowledge given that the Lord delivered both Noah and Lot from the judgement that came upon the rest of the world at that time. We know that God's wrath will be released a final time very soon, but again we can rest assured knowing that He will deliver us from this final time of judgement and bring us safely to His kingdom.

## January 19

> For this very reason, make every effort to supplement your faith with virtue, and virtue with knowledge, and knowledge with self-control, and self-control with steadfastness, and steadfastness with godliness, and godliness with brotherly affection, and brotherly affection with love. 2 Peter 1:5-7

We all need to eat a healthy diet in order to stay in good shape and sometimes it's helpful to take supplements to add nutrients and minerals to our body alongside the food we are eating. Peter makes it clear that it's the same in the spiritual. We are saved by faith in Jesus Christ alone, but in order to make our calling and election to God's heavenly kingdom sure, we must supplement our faith with the qualities listed above and if we practise them daily, we can be assured that we are becoming more like Jesus and will be welcomed by Him into glory.

## January 20

> The LORD of hosts will reign on Mount Zion and in Jerusalem and before His elders, gloriously. Isaiah 24:23.

This chapter starts off with a great announcement of coming judgement upon the earth which will be fulfilled in the Great Tribulation period. This will be a terrible time of distress and desolation in which a third of mankind will perish for the sins of the world. In the midst of this great upheaval and shaking though there will be people that acknowledge and turn to the Lord and praise Him singing "Glory to the Righteous One" (Isaiah 24:16). Then Jesus will return and will usher in a glorious new era where He is Lord over all the earth and we are His people forever. Maranatha, Come Lord Jesus!

## January 21

> Behold, the LORD will hurl you away violently, O you strong man...I will thrust you from your office, and you will be pulled down from your station. Isaiah 22:17,19

I've had warning visions and dreams for leaders of nations over the past few years and have seen some of them come to pass in a short space of time. The above passage is a warning to any leader who rules in defiance of God and who acts corruptly. All of us will stand before God and have to give an account of our lives from the greatest to the least and no one will escape. Pray for leaders today that they would turn to the Lord and fear Him and that righteousness would abound in our lands. God doesn't want anyone to perish.

## January 22

> In that day I will call my servant Eliakim the son of Hilkiah, and I will clothe him with your robe, and will bind your sash on him, and will commit your authority to his hand. And he shall be a father to the inhabitants of Jerusalem and to the house of Judah. And I will place on his shoulder the key of the house of David. He shall open, and none shall shut; and he shall shut, and none shall open. Isaiah 22:20-22.

Yesterday we saw a warning to ungodly leaders but today we see a promise of promotion to those who follow the Lord and serve Him uprightly. Eliakim replaced the leader whom God removed and was given "the key of the house of David" which meant he had access to the whole kingdom! As followers and coheirs with Christ, we too now have full access to all that God has prepared for those who love Him and can walk in His authority as kings and priests.

## January 23

*But if you do not drive out the inhabitants of the land from before you, then those of them whom you let remain shall be as barbs in your eyes and thorns in your sides, and they shall trouble you in the land where you dwell. Numbers 33:55*

This was quite a sobering warning from God about driving out every last enemy from the land. This is true for us today as His people. Christ has redeemed us from sin and death and made us the righteousness of God in Himself but we still have a duty to get rid of any wrong habit or practice that we used to do. If we don't then it'll trip us up as we try to run our race and will affect our spiritual growth. Ask the Lord to show you anything that still remains in your life that shouldn't be there and ask Him to remove it by His Spirit.

## January 24

*The centurion replied, "Lord, I do not deserve to have you come under my roof. But just say the word, and my servant will be healed. Matthew 8:8*

The centurion needed a miracle and quickly for his paralysed and suffering servant and he knew that one word from Jesus would be enough. He was right, for as soon as Jesus declared healing it was done at that very moment. If you need a miracle and touch from heaven today then ask the Lord to speak the word over your life and situation and believe by faith that it is done for His word will not return without accomplishing its mission.

## January 25

There is no fear in love, but perfect love casts out fear. For fear has to do with punishment, and whoever fears has not been perfected in love. I John 4:18.

According to the apostle John, fear comes from the absence of love. If someone is walking in the perfect love of God then there should be no reason to fear. How do we know God's love? The key is found in verse 16: "God is love, and whoever abides in love abides in God, and God abides in him." The Greek word for abide is menó and means to wait, remain, love, continue, endure. The more we remain in God's word and presence then the more we will remain in His love and the less we will succumb to fear. Also if we love others we will abide in God's love.

## January 26

Then Pharaoh gave this order to all his people: "Every Hebrew boy that is born you must throw into the Nile, but let every girl live." Exodus 1:22

I was recently invited to a meeting by a Christian legal organisation that fights against anti-Christian laws in the UK and it shared the shocking statistics of abortion around the world. The spirit of Pharaoh is sadly still operative and wants to destroy the next generation of children made in the image of God. Praise God for those who are standing against this heinous crime whether at a legal level or in prayer. Nothing is impossible with God, as was seen with the overturning of Roe v's Wade in America in June 2022. As followers of Jesus we must do everything we can to promote and save life, for the devil wants to steal, kill and destroy but Christ came to give life in abundance.

## January 27

*God heard their groaning and he remembered his covenant with Abraham, with Isaac and with Jacob. So God looked on the Israelites and was concerned about them. Exodus 2:24-25*

My children can play happily in another room on their own for a while until they either get bored and look for something else to do or one of them gets upset. When I hear a cry of distress or consistent annoyance then I know that it's time to check on them and intervene. The same is true of God. When a certain cry from His people reaches His ears, He cannot help but take action. This was illustrated by the parable of the persistent widow who kept pleading with the judge for justice until she got it and Jesus told us to be like her in our prayers for divine help. Don't stop asking the Lord for His help in your life and situation today, for He will come through.

## January 28

*Be merciful to those who doubt; save others by snatching them from the fire; to others show mercy, mixed with fear—hating even the clothing stained by corrupted flesh. Jude 1:22-23.*

As we build our faith in the Lord, we will be in a better position to help others and Jude shows us how we can respond to those who are struggling. We can show God's mercy to those with unbelief, just as we have been shown mercy and we can pull others out of the darkness and into His Kingdom when the opportunity arises. Ask God to use you in this way whether it is with family, friends, neighbours or colleagues. There is a world to reach right now.

## January 29

"Now then, please let your servant remain here as my lord's slave in place of the boy, and let the boy return with his brothers."
Genesis 44:33

Judah was willing to lay down his life for Benjamin and it showed that he had truly transformed since selling Joseph into slavery many years before. Jesus, who was from the tribe of Judah, was not only willing to lay down his life for us, but did so when He willingly went to the cross. John 15:13 says, "Greater love has no one than this: to lay down one's life for one's friends." The more we follow the Lord and become like Him, the more we will put the needs of others before our own. Jesus was able to give His life in exchange for ours because He saw the joy of us being with Him together in glory forever. When we grasp the exceeding greatness of what God has prepared for us in heaven and walk in His infinite love, then it will become much easier to lay our lives down for others.


## January 30

To him who is able to keep you from stumbling and to present you before his glorious presence without fault and with great joy—to the only God our Saviour be glory, majesty, power and authority, through Jesus Christ our Lord, before all ages, now and forevermore! Amen. Jude 1;24-25.

There are certain scriptures in the bible that we can take and hold onto as life verses to continually meditate on and memorise while we live on the earth. This is one of them, for it is a powerful reminder that God, who calls us to be holy and set apart, is able to bring us through every trial and temptation so that we can stand before Him in glory unblemished at the end of our lives.

# January 31

*So Joseph settled his father and his brothers in Egypt and gave them property in the best part of the land, the district of Rameses, as Pharaoh directed. Genesis 47:11*

Do you need a house or home today? Do not doubt God but believe He can provide for you even in difficult financial times. The earth belongs to the Lord and He can give it to whoever He wants to and He wants to provide places of rest for us to live in. I recently heard that some friends of ours who also serve God in the UK were given a house to own by someone completely free of charge! What God can do for one, He is able to do for another, so if this is your need today, keep believing and thanking Him for miraculous and supernatural provision.

## February 1

I know your works. Behold, I have set before you an open door, which no one is able to shut. I know that you have but little power, and yet you have kept my word and have not denied my name.
Revelation 3:8

God is in control of the doors in our lives. When He opens a door, no one can shut it and when He closes a door, no one can open it. It is up to us though whether we will go through the open doors in front of us or hang around the doors that have closed. The enemy will try to resist us going through the doors that God opens but he cannot stop us. If you see a divine opportunity from the Lord today, take it and go through it into all that He has stored up for you on the other side. It'll be worth it.

## February 2

Love the Lord your God with all your heart and with all your soul and with all your strength. Deuteronomy 6:5

Moses told the people to love God above everything else, for in doing so it would lead to the fulfilment of the other commandments. If we can truly love God with everything then we will not be unfaithful to Him and we will be able to walk in holiness as He wants us to. It will also help us to carry out the second great commandment to love others as ourselves and which according to Romans 13:10 is the very fulfilment of God's law. Ask the Holy Spirit to help you walk in love today from beginning to end, even when it is difficult to do so.

## February 3

> Then the commander stood and called out in Hebrew, "Hear the words of the great king, the king of Assyria! This is what the king says: Do not let Hezekiah deceive you. He cannot deliver you! Do not let Hezekiah persuade you to trust in the Lord when he says, 'The Lord will surely deliver us; this city will not be given into the hand of the king of Assyria.' Isaiah 35:13-15

This commander was a high ranking military officer in the Assyrian army and he was using intimidation tactics to force the people of Jerusalem to surrender to them. In a similar way, the devil sends high ranking demons to intimidate and entice families and churches to give in to temptation and pressure, thinking that it's better to give up than to keep going forward. Do not listen to the enemy's lies but listen entirely to the voice and word of God for He will surely deliver us from the hand of the enemy every time we call out to Him.

## February 4

> Then will the lame leap like a deer, and the mute tongue shout for joy. Water will gush forth in the wilderness and streams in the desert. Isaiah 35:6

This is a wonderful chapter that promises great blessing, abundance and freedom to God's people as they trust in Him. It promises that those who feel immobilised in their Christian walk will suddenly have the power to leap like a deer and shout for joy. Deer have been known to jump as high as 8 to 10 feet and some are able to leap up and climb steep mountains and hills. This is what we can do in the power of the Holy Spirit as we abide in Him. Let this year become a "leap" year as you supernaturally jump with joy over every hurdle and obstacle that the enemy puts in front of you.

## February 5

Then I took the sinful thing, the calf that you had made, and burned it with fire and crushed it, grinding it very small, until it was as fine as dust. And I threw the dust of it into the brook that ran down from the mountain. Deuteronomy 9:21

God hates sin and we are to hate it as much as He does. Sometimes we are able to instantly give up certain sins and strongholds and other times it can take longer, for they are more embedded and need to be gradually dismantled and overcome. When this is the case, don't stop attacking that weak area, but continue to break it down through prayer, fasting and the word and eventually it'll become so small that it'll disappear and cease to exist and you'll forget it was ever there!

## February 6

Hezekiah received the letter from the hand of the messengers, and read it; and Hezekiah went up to the house of the LORD, and spread it before the LORD. And Hezekiah prayed to the LORD. Isaiah 37:14-15.

There will be times when we receive a bad report of some kind. Our natural reaction is probably to take it at face value and believe what it says, but this is not faith. Instead we should take it to God like king Hezekiah and ask Him to take care of it no matter how intimidating it is, for there is nothing too hard for the Lord. 1 Peter 5:7 describes this as "casting all your care upon Him, for He cares for you." Try doing this the next time you receive some bad news.

## February 7

Love the Lord your God and keep his requirements, his decrees, his laws and his commands always. Deuteronomy 11:1.

I recently preached a message on loving God and said that it is one of the most important things to do as a Christian. The Bible describes it as the greatest commandant and the second is to love our neighbour as ourselves. It is the key to holiness for if we truly love others then it shows that God's love is in us and we will have fulfilled the law. It also drives out fear, for 1 John 4:18 says, "There is no fear in love. But perfect love drives out fear."

## February 8

Then the word of the Lord came to Isaiah: "Go and tell Hezekiah, 'This is what the Lord, the God of your father David, says: I have heard your prayer and seen your tears; I will add fifteen years to your life. And I will deliver you and this city from the hand of the king of Assyria. I will defend this city. Isaiah 38:4-6.

Yesterday we saw how God gave Moses a second chance to receive and pass on the ten commandments to the people of Israel. Here we see God give king Hezekiah another chance at life itself after telling him that he was going to die. If you feel like your life or purpose is over then do what Hezekiah did and begin to pray and ask God for mercy and grace to fulfil what He has called you to do while here on the earth and then you'll also be able to say "You restored me to health and let me live.. .you have put all my sins behind your back" (Isaiah 38:16-17).

## February 9

At that time the Lord said to me, "Chisel out two stone tablets like the first ones and come up to me on the mountain. Also make a wooden ark. I will write on the tablets the words that were on the first tablets, which you broke. Then you are to put them in the ark." Deuteronomy 10:1-2.

Do you need another chance at something? We serve a God of the second chance. He is merciful and long suffering and is willing to give us another opportunity even if we messed it up the first time. Moses had fasted food and water for forty days and nights while face to face with the Lord on Mount Sinai and God had divinely inscribed the ten commandments on two tablets which Moses broke on returning to the camp, but here he is given another chance to get it right. Is there something broken in your life today - a relationship, career, mission, hope, or something else? Ask God for another chance to get it right and by His grace you will.

## February 10

...but those who hope in the Lord will renew their strength. They will soar on wings like eagles; they will run and not grow weary, they will walk and not be faint. Isaiah 40:31

There is a supernatural strength and grace that comes from spending time with the Lord. It defies natural ability and energy and gives us power to serve God whatever our age. Many Christian ministers and believers have continued building the kingdom beyond retirement age and achieved some of their most fruitful work later on in life. Don't let age or aches stop you from stepping out today, but let the Holy Spirit take you on a new adventure as you wait upon Him.

## February 11

> Shout for joy to the Lord, all the earth. Worship the Lord with gladness; come before him with joyful songs. Psalm 100:1-2

Following the Lord should not be dreary, boring or sober. If it is then it is probably religion and not a Christ-centred, vibrant and living faith! We should be the happiest and hopeful people on the planet because we serve a great and awesome God who loves us and who has redeemed us from sin and death forever. This is why Paul and Silas were able to praise loudly even after they had been beaten and put in prison. Don't let anything stop you from joyful singing and rejoicing today.

## February 12

> However, there need be no poor people among you, for in the land the Lord your God is giving you to possess as your inheritance, he will richly bless you, if only you fully obey the Lord your God and are careful to follow all these commands I am giving you today. Deuteronomy 15:4-5

This is a powerful promise of God's provision. While our aim in life should be to store up treasure in heaven and not to accumulate as much as we can on the earth, we can still expect the Lord to provide for our daily needs. From my own experience, the more I have sought to follow Him and walk in His ways, the more I have experienced His blessing upon my life and have not had to strive outside of Him. If you have a need today then bring it before God and trust that He will meet it as you look to Him as your provider.

## February 13

If any of your people—Hebrew men or women—sell themselves to you and serve you six years, in the seventh year you must let them go free. Deuteronomy 15:12.

Life in ancient Israel was marked by cycles of seven years and the seventh year was special. Any outstanding debts were to be forgiven and let go of. Slaves could walk away free after six years of service and the land itself was to be left alone so that it could enjoy a sabbatical year of rest from agriculture. The number seven represents completion and so God recognised the seventh year as a chance to finish one season or cycle and start again in a better way. He offers us the same new beginning as we put our faith in Jesus and follow Him today.

## February 14

For God so loved the world that he gave his one and only Son, that whoever believes in him shall not perish but have eternal life. John 3:16

Today is Valentine's day and many couples will buy each other a gift or enjoy a meal together to celebrate their love. True love though begins with God. 1 John 4:16 tells us that "God is love" and Romans 5:8 makes a powerful statement when it says, "But God demonstrates his own love for us in this: While we were still sinners, Christ died for us." In order to really love God, ourselves and others, we first need to receive God's love and accept the demonstration of His love by believing in Jesus and receiving the forgiveness that He provided for us. For "greater love has no one than this: to lay down one's life for one's friends" (John 15:13) and that is exactly what Christ did for us.

## February 15

*...the accuser of our brothers and sisters, who accuses them before our God day and night, has been hurled down." Revelation 12:10*

The name Satan means accuser or adversary. One of his biggest strategies is to oppose God's people by reminding them of their past sins and mistakes. You have probably experienced this many times when the enemy has told you that you are unworthy and sinful and bound by a particular weakness or sin. The good news is that Christ defeated Satan and all his accusations at the cross and we can now cast down every evil imagination and lie and make it obey Jesus instead of harassing us. We are the righteousness of God in Christ and must remind the devil of this every time he tells us the opposite.

## February 16

*They triumphed over him by the blood of the Lamb and by the word of their testimony; they did not love their lives so much as to shrink from death. Revelation 12:11*

Yesterday we learnt that Satan comes to accuse and harass us as God's chosen people and now we can discover the tools for standing against his attacks in the very next verse. There are three powerful weapons at our disposal at all times: pleading and applying the precious blood of Jesus - especially in taking communion and appropriating what Jesus has done, declaring what Christ has already done for us and then finally dying to the demands of our flesh and coming alive in Him, so that this world has no more hold on us. We can and will triumph as we put these weapons to work.

## February 17

> Observe the month of Aviv and celebrate the Passover of the LORD your God, because in the month of Aviv he brought you out of Egypt by night. Deuteronomy 16:1

The Israelites were told to observe the entire month of Aviv on the Hebrew calendar and to celebrate the Passover. The Hebrew word for observe means to watch, to keep, to guard, like a watchman or doorkeeper. God warned them to always be attentive during this time because this would be when the greatest sacrifice of all history would be made when Jesus died on the cross. In a similar way, we must now observe and be watchful for Christ's return which could happen at any time.

## February 18

> "Forget the former things; do not dwell on the past. See, I am doing a new thing! Now it springs up; do you not perceive it? I am making a way in the wilderness and streams in the wasteland. Isaiah 43:18-19.

Recently I shared a prophetic word that God was doing a new thing and the very next day it was my reading! When God tells us to forget the past, He means it, because we will not be able to fully perceive and embrace the new thing that He is doing if we continue holding onto old ways and attitudes. This is why Israel didn't recognise Jesus as the Messiah at His advent for they were too fixed on the Mosaic law and the Old Covenant. Open your heart to what God wants to do differently in your life today.

## February 19

> And I saw a beast rising out of the sea, with ten horns and seven heads, with ten diadems on its horns and blasphemous names on its heads. Revelation 13:1.

We know that the devil can only imitate and not create like God can so it stands to reason that he will mimic the Trinity in the last days. The dragon in Revelation 12 is the opposite to God the Father, the first beast is the opposite to God the Son and the second beast is the opposite to God the Holy Spirit. Just as the Spirit leads people to accept and worship Jesus, the second beast or false prophet will cause people to worship the first beast or antichrist. Praise God for a real Saviour in Jesus Christ today - the name above all names!

## February 20

> ...who carries out the words of his servants and fulfills the predictions of his messengers. Isaiah 44:26

The spoken prophetic word is very powerful when it comes to pass. I've received words from the Lord over the years both directly from Him and from others and when it happens it is life-giving. If God's word is still to be outworked in your life then hold on and do not lose faith for it will surely come about at the right time and you'll be ready to step into it when it does. The word of God never returns to Him void but always accomplishes the purpose that it was sent out to do.

# February 21

> Then I looked, and there before me was the Lamb, standing on Mount Zion, and with him 144,000 who had his name and his Father's name written on their foreheads. Revelation 14:1

We read Revelation 13:1 a couple of days ago which describes the rise of the antichrist and false prophet and the mark of the beast. You could say that this will be the climax of evil in the world and what's interesting is that the number 13 is often linked with rebellion, evil or sin. In the next chapter though, chapter 14, we read about Jesus, the Lamb of God and those who will follow Him in the last days in the midst of all the evil and who will be delivered from the earth. The number 14 is connected with deliverance and so is appropriate here. Even in the midst of great darkness and trials, the Lord will rescue us, His chosen people, when we cry out to Him.

# February 22

> I saw in heaven another great and marvelous sign: seven angels with the seven last plagues. Revelation 15:1.

The number 7 in the bible represents completion and so it's fitting that 7 angels are released to bring the judgement of God to a conclusion. God's wrath is poured out on those who have consistently rejected Jesus as their Lord and Saviour. The Lord is patient and long suffering with those who do not acknowledge or worship Him, but He also promised that this current, sinful and corrupted world age would come to an end. As believers, we know this time is coming very soon. Pray for those who do not know Christ today and boldly share the good news of salvation with them.

## February 23

*Even to your old age and gray hairs I am he, I am he who will sustain you. I have made you and I will carry you; I will sustain you and I will rescue you. Isaiah 46:4*

This comforting promise is available for all of us today. Our only requirement is to believe, follow and obey the Lord Jesus Christ. He cares for us as the good shepherd and when we find it hard to go on in life, He will carry us in His arms through every difficulty, danger and trial. After four decades of following Christ and having been rescued on many occasions, I can testify to the faithfulness of God and can assure you that He will be with us till the very end.

## February 24

*When you go to war against your enemies and see horses and chariots and an army greater than yours, do not be afraid of them, because the Lord your God...will be with you. Deuteronomy 20:1*

Yesterday I watched a movie about the 1973 Yom Kippur war. The neighbouring enemies of Israel tried to invade the nation with a surprise attack involving large numbers of soldiers and weaponry. Despite the odds, Israel fought back and was victorious in less than three weeks. This isn't the first attack God's nation has encountered and won't be the last. On 7 October 2023, almost 50 years to the day, enemy forces launched another surprise attack, but again Israel has fought back and gained the upper hand. God has promised to watch over Israel forever, so no matter how many foes try to invade the country, God will continue to defend it right till the end and He will fight for us till the end of our lives also.

## February 25

> ...the world will be astonished when they see the beast, because it once was, now is not, and yet will come. Rev 17:8

The final beast system described in the book of Revelation will be a revival of the Roman Empire. It existed, disappeared but is now emerging again. In 1957, six European nations came together and signed the treaty of Rome which paved the way for the current EU. Global events right now are helping to strengthen the power and influence of the EU on the world stage and eventually it will even overtake America as the leading superpower and dominant political and military force. The good news though is that God is raising up His church in Europe at this time to be ready for a mighty harvest of souls before the end.

## February 26

> This is what the Lord says—your Redeemer, the Holy One of Israel: "I am the Lord your God, who teaches you what is best for you, who directs you in the way you should go." Isaiah 48:17

There are two great promises in this verse: the Lord will show us where to go and what to do for our good. He knows what we need and where we can find it and if we take the time to pray and listen to Him, then He can open new streams of income and opportunity. I remember needing a large space for a new business I had just set up and after praying about it, I heard two words unexpectedly. After consulting another Christian about a possible venue, he told me that he couldn't help me but suggested trying the name that I had heard in prayer. It turned out to be available and perfect for what I needed and God's favour was on it from beginning to end. Ask the Holy Spirit today to show you what you need to know.

## February 27

*Rejoice over her, you heavens! Rejoice, you people of God! Rejoice, apostles and prophets! For God has judged her with the judgement she imposed on you. Revelation 18:20*

Here John is talking about the final end-time Babylon which we know represents the dominating world government, economy and system outside of God. It has always existed in some form ever since the tower of Babel and it will reach its peak in the tribulation period with excessive luxury and splendour, before being destroyed by the Lord in just one hour never to recover again. God will judge it for its many sins especially for its persecution of the saints. Don't be led astray by the spirit of this world today but keep your eyes on Jesus and the heavenly Jerusalem that awaits us as believers in glory.

## February 28

*He provides food for those who fear him; he remembers his covenant forever. Psalm 111:5*

The Lord knows what we need and when we need it and will provide for our needs. Do not fear lack or going without for He has promised to never leave us nor forsake us for all our lives. I'm always amazed at how God can come through at the last minute and answer our prayers whether it is for food, money, clothing, a tax bill, rent, a home, a vehicle, a church, a friend or a spouse. Trust God to be your source today and thank Him for the answer by faith before it comes along.

# February 29

*Your troops will be willing on your day of battle. Arrayed in holy splendour, your young men will come to you like dew from the morning's womb. Psalms 110:3*

Earlier this month, I had two back to back dreams about a large evangelistic ministry setting up a unique venture here in Scotland. By the end of the dream, I was in a large room with lots of other evangelists as this new work was launched. I then woke up and read Psalm 110. God is calling us today to be willing vessels for His kingdom and to go into the world and share the good news about Jesus. We can all play a part in this even if it means reaching one person in our neighbourhood with God's love.

## March 1

*However, the Lord your God would not listen to Balaam but turned the curse into a blessing for you, because the Lord your God loves you. Deuteronomy 23:5*

Do not be afraid of people trying to curse you today. Proverbs 26:2 assures us that an undeserved curse does not come to rest. When we are walking with the Lord and doing what is right before Him then it doesn't matter if people talk about us behind our back or slander us, for their words will not find a place to land. Instead God is able to turn those words into a blessing and vindicate us from what has been said about us. God's truth always prevails and He will deliver us from every accusation and lie.

## March 2

*He who vindicates me is near. Who then will bring charges against me? Let us face each other! Who is my accuser? Let him confront me! Isaiah 50:8*

We know that Satan means accuser and one of his primary roles is to continually accuse us before God and remind us of our past. Thank God we have an advocate in Jesus who has forgiven us of our sins and declared us righteous before the Father. We can now talk back to the accuser and refuse to accept his lies and charges. If the devil is harassing you today with wrong thoughts or words then remind him that you are are forgiven, accepted and saved and that his lies have no place in your life.

# March 3

*Blessed and holy are those who share in the first resurrection. The second death has no power over them, but they will be priests of God and of Christ and will reign with him for a thousand years. Revelation 20:6.*

As soon as Christ returns to the earth which we believe is very soon then it will initiate the millennial reign or one thousand years of peace on the earth. Jesus will reign as King from Jerusalem, the Jewish people will all worship and follow Him and believers will be resurrected to live and reign on the earth. There will be no more disease or suffering and God will fulfil promises during this period to Jesus, Israel, believers and the world. It will be a glorious time before we live in the new heavens and the new earth forever.

# March 4

*The cowering prisoners will soon be set free; they will not die in their dungeon, nor will they lack bread. Isaiah 51:14*

What a promise! The Lord will deliver us at just the right time. The ESV adds speedily. So many of us can feel like a spiritual prisoner, bound by sickness, anxiety, fear, lack and much more. It is the enemy's plan to imprison every human soul, but Jesus came to set the captives free. Do not believe the lie that you will always have to suffer in the way that you are right now, but look to the Lord for freedom and deliverance for it's your inheritance and birthright today!

# March 5

He who was seated on the throne said, "I am making everything new!" Then he said, "Write this down, for these words are trustworthy and true." Revelation 21:5

One day God is going to remake the heavens and the earth and everything around us will be brand new. No longer will we think about past regrets, pain, trauma or loss, but we will focus entirely on the Lord and worship Him for saving us and redeeming us and making us citizens of heaven. We can begin to experience this newness of life now in Jesus for 2 Corinthians 5:17 promises us that "if anyone is in Christ, the new creation has come: the old has gone, the new is here!"

# March 6

How beautiful on the mountains are the feet of those who bring good news, who proclaim peace, who bring good tidings, who proclaim salvation, who say to Zion, "Your God reigns!" Isaiah 52:7

Our feet will lead us to do good or bad. Proverbs 1:16 says that the feet of sinful people rush into evil, whereas Isaiah sees the feet of those who share the gospel and good news of Jesus as blessed and beautiful. I like this analogy because I enjoy walking regularly for exercise and sunlight and I often try to share the gospel at the same time as the opportunity arises. The apostle Paul may have had this in mind also when he told us to put on the shoes of peace, for the gospel shows the world how to make peace with God through faith in Jesus Christ. This is the good news that we can all take with us today.

## March 7

> But he was pierced for our transgressions, he was crushed for our iniquities; the punishment that brought us peace was on him, and by his wounds we are healed. Issue 53:5

This must be one of the most precious verses in the bible. Jesus was beaten and punished so that we could be forgiven and healed. There is no other god or religion that offers this. Instead it's usually about what we can do in order to please God and find salvation. "But God demonstrates his own love for us in this: While we were still sinners, Christ died for us" (Romans 5:8). No wonder the name of Jesus is now the name above every other name and that one day every knee will bow before Him and declare that He is Lord!

## March 8

> If you fully obey the Lord your God and carefully follow all his commands I give you today, the Lord your God will set you high above all the nations on earth. All these blessings will come on you and accompany you if you obey the Lord your God. Deuteronomy 28:1-2

Israel had a choice whether to follow the Lord and obey Him or not. If they did then they could expect to be greatly blessed beyond measure. If they didn't then the opposite would result and it would bring a great curse upon them. God's first and foremost plan is to bless us and set us on high but it takes our cooperation and willingness. We must be willing to fully obey Him in all things and this is only possible through the help and power of the Holy Spirit. Ask the Holy Spirit for God's grace today to become more like Jesus and walk in His ways so that His promise of blessing can be yours.

## March 9

"Sing, barren woman, you who never bore a child; burst into song, shout for joy, you who were never in labour; because more are the children of the desolate woman than of her who has a husband," says the Lord. Isaiah 54:1

Isaiah 54 is such a powerful and life-giving chapter that it should be read, studied and reread. It contains so many great promises of increase, expansion and restoration. It would not be possible though without the preceding chapter which points out the suffering that Jesus would endure for us so that we could enter into this greater covenant of healing, fruitfulness, joy and peace. Don't forget to thank the Lord today for all that He has done and continues to do in your life as you follow Him.

## March 10

"Enlarge the place of your tent, stretch your tent curtains wide, do not hold back; lengthen your cords, strengthen your stakes. For you will spread out to the right and to the left; your descendants will dispossess nations and settle in their desolate cities." Isaiah 54:2-3

If God promises to make us fruitful and take away our spiritual barrenness then we will naturally need to make room for all that He will give us. This starts in our minds. If we can take hold of the words of the Lord by faith and hold onto them until we see them then there will eventually be an outworking of what God said He would do. Ask the Holy Spirit for fresh vision today to see all that God has for you and for the faith to believe for increase and multiplication in every area of your life. He does not want us to settle for the least.

## March 11

*The Lord will send on you curses, confusion and rebuke in everything you put your hand to...because of the evil you have done in forsaking him. Deuteronomy 28:20*

God promised great blessings to Israel if they followed Him and kept His commandments. He also warned them of great curses if they disobeyed Him and served other gods. Likewise we have a daily choice to walk with the Lord and not reject Him. Now that we have committed our lives to Him there is no turning back. When we try to go back to our old lives and old habits and ways then it's never the same and is usually much worse for us than when we were living without Christ in the world. Make a decision today to keep going forward with Jesus no matter what happens and leave the past behind. You are now a new creation in Christ and the old has gone. Amen!

## March 12

*Then the devil left him, and angels came and attended him. Matthew 4:11*

We will all be tempted and tested in this life and there is no escaping it for its part and parcel of the Christian walk, but it will not last forever. In the midst of the trial it might feel like it will never end but we have to remember that there is always an end date to what we are going through. Even Jesus was tempted by the devil but when he stood His ground and refused to give in, the enemy gave up and left and angels were quickly dispatched instead to minister to Jesus' needs. If you're being tempted or tested today, humble yourself before God and resist the devil and he will have to flee!

# March 13

Now choose life, so that you and your children may live and that you may love the Lord your God, listen to his voice, and hold fast to him. Deuteronomy 30:19-20

God has always been about freedom and life whereas the devil likes to enslave people and ultimately destroy them. The more of the Lord we have in our life, the more freedom and liberty we will experience no matter what our external circumstances are, but the more we listen to the enemy the more bound we will be. This is why Moses warned us to stay close to God and keep His commandments all our lives so that we would be blessed and not cursed. We can achieve this today by following and obeying Jesus Christ who came to fulfil the law for us.

# March 14

Then Moses commanded them: "At the end of every seven years, in the year for cancelling debts, during the Festival of Tabernacles, when all Israel comes to appear before the Lord your God at the place he will choose, you shall read this law before them in their hearing. Deuteronomy 31:10-11.

The final seventh year was to be a Sabbath rest for the land and a time of release from debts owed. This gave the people and ground a time to reset. It was called the Shemitah and means the year of release. At the very end of this time, the Levites were to read the law of God to the people. This reminded them how to live and what their purpose was going into the next season. If you're going into a new season or chapter of your life then enter it with God's word and let it guide you in the way you should go.

# March 15

*...then your light will rise in the darkness, and your night will become like the noon day. The Lord will guide you always; he will satisfy your needs in a sun-scorched land and will strengthen your frame. Isaiah 58:10-11*

Isaiah 58 talks about the true fast that God commends and approves of. The people of this time were fasting food and appearing humble, but were still mistreating family and workers, breaking the Sabbath and failing to help and bless the poor. It was an empty religious ritual devoid of God's heart. Fasting is good and we should try and incorporate it into our lives, but at the same time, God wants us to have a true heart change towards Him and towards those around us so that we seek to bless others and not harm them. If we do this then we can expect to walk in divine blessing as the Lord promised.

# March 16

*"As for me, this is my covenant with them," says the Lord. "My Spirit, who is on you, will not depart from you, and my words that I have put in your mouth will always be on your lips...says the Lord. Isaiah 59:21*

We need both the Spirit and the word to be effective Christians. If we just have the word then we will become dry and lack revelation without the Spirit. If we just have the Spirit then we will be in danger of not walking in the truth of God's word and will be open to emotions and feelings more than scripture. If we have both the Spirit and the word then we can expect to walk in divine power and understanding and see God move in greater ways. Ask Him today for both in your life.

## March 17

*If you, then, though you are evil, know how to give good gifts to your children, how much more will your Father in heaven give good gifts to those who ask him! Matthew 7:11*

Faith will lead us to come boldly before God's throne of grace in our hour of need. We are not called to be shy and introverted Christians who are afraid to ask for help, provision or direction. God is ready and willing to help us, provide for us and guide us but we need to ask, seek and knock. We serve a loving heavenly Father who wants to give us the best of His kingdom today so go ahead and ask for good gifts.

## March 18

*Moses was a hundred and twenty years old when he died, yet his eyes were not weak nor his strength gone. Deuteronomy 34:7*

We do not need to settle for infirmity or premature death. God has promised a full life span for us as a blessing for obedience and faith in Him. Jesus died on the cross for both sin and sickness and all throughout the bible there are promises of healing and wholeness. Psalm 103:3-4 tells us that it is God who heals all our diseases and who redeems our life from the pit. Isaiah 53:5 promises us that by his wounds we are healed. Declare that God is your healer today and that you don't have to grow old with aches, pains and other age-related issues, but can walk in supernatural life and health.

## March 19

> Be strong and very courageous. Be careful to obey all the law my servant Moses gave you; do not turn from it to the right or to the left, that you may be successful wherever you go. Keep this Book of the Law always on your lips; meditate on it day and night, so that you may be careful to do everything written in it. Then you will be prosperous and successful. Joshua 1:7-8

The key to kingdom success in this life is to live according to God's word. It is our road map and source of wisdom and knowledge for everything we will encounter. The Jewish people understand this and speak the word everyday in synagogues and homes and as a result have been a prosperous and successful people over the centuries. Make a commitment this year to read, declare and memorise the bible daily and watch the blessing it will bring.

## March 20

> The Spirit of the Sovereign Lord is on me, because the Lord has anointed me to proclaim good news to the poor. He has sent me to bind up the brokenhearted, to proclaim freedom for the captives and release from darkness for the prisoners. Isaiah 61:1

Yesterday I talked about the importance of reading and even memorising God's word. Isaiah 61:1-3 is a passage that is worth learning by heart for it was the very mission and mandate of Jesus when he lived on the earth and it is now our mission as we partner with the Holy Spirit. When God touches our lives and fills us up then we will want to go and share His love and freedom with others and the Spirit will enable us to be effective in doing this.

## March 21

*"Agreed," she replied. "Let it be as you say." So she sent them away, and they departed. And she tied the scarlet cord in the window. Joshua 2:21*

As soon as Rahab had been told that she and her household would be saved from destruction if she put a scarlet cord in the window of her home, she went and put it on display without delay. The scarlet cord was a foreshadow of the blood of Jesus that saves all who put their trust in it's redeeming power. Like the blood on the Israelites' doorposts in Egypt, the scarlet cord would deliver everyone inside the home when God's judgement came to the city of Jericho. We must be like Rahab and immediately apply the blood of Jesus to our homes, families and lives for only His precious blood will save us from the forces of darkness against us and the consequences of sin.

## March 22

*"When you see the ark of the covenant of the Lord your God...you are to move out from your positions and follow it. Then you will know which way to go...Joshua 3:3-4*

There have been times in my life when I've been ready to move in a certain direction but then God has led me on another route and it's proved right. Isaiah 30:21 says, "Whether you turn to the right or to the left, your ears will hear a voice behind you, saying, "This is the way; walk in it." God has promised to guide us by His Holy Spirit but we need to be moving first in order to be led. Fix your eyes on Jesus today and start moving towards Him and trust Him to lead you in paths of righteousness for His name sake!

## March 23

> "Come to me, all you who are weary and burdened, and I will give you rest. Take my yoke upon you and learn from me, for I am gentle and humble in heart, and you will find rest for your souls. For my yoke is easy and my burden is light." Matthew 11:28-30

What a great promise we have from God! Firstly, there is an invitation to come to Him in our stress and weakness. Secondly, He will not only accept and receive us but will give us the rest we so desperately need. Thirdly, His teaching and words will be the yoke that gives us peace for oxen in ancient times were led by the yoke on their shoulders and likewise we will find true and lasting contentment as we follow Him and are led by Him.

## March 24

> But I tell you that everyone will have to give account on the day of judgement for every empty word they have spoken. For by your words you will be acquitted, and by your words you will be condemned. Matthew 12:36-37

Words come from the overflow of the heart and reveal what we are thinking, feeling and meditating on. If our hearts are not right then our words will reflect this in our speech and we will say things that we later regret. This is why it's important to walk in faith and keep a right heart attitude so that we can be ready to say something uplifting and faith-building like "I can do all things through Christ who strengthens me" and "I am the righteousness of God in Christ no matter what the enemy says about me!" Let God's words dwell in your heart today so that they naturally overflow from your mouth when you open it.

# March 25

*The day after the Passover...they ate some of the produce of the land...The manna stopped the day after they ate this food from the land. Joshua 5:11-12*

The Israelites were supernaturally fed with manna in the wilderness for forty years by God, but as soon as they had crossed over into the Promised Land and celebrated Passover, they began to eat the produce of the land instead and the manna stopped. The nation went from being fed from heaven to feeding themselves from the land that God had given them. We must never be afraid of a source of provision drying up for if one stream ends, God is more than able to open another one in its place. The Lord is our provider and has promised to never leave us nor forsake us all the days of our lives.

# March 26

*"The kingdom of heaven is like a mustard seed...Though it is the smallest of all seeds, yet when it grows, it is the largest of garden plants and becomes a tree." Matthew 13:31-32*

Do not be afraid of starting small in whatever you are doing. Most things in life have to begin small and then grow as they progress. Humans, animals, plants, trees, cities and nations all begin as a seed but then get bigger as they develop. It is the same with our faith. We all start out with a similar measure of faith but as we walk with the Lord, our faith enlarges as we see God work in our lives and come through for us even in difficult times. What looks insignificant today could become something influential in the future so don't give up on what the Lord has called you to do right now - it can grow!

## March 27

*The seventh time around, when the priests sounded the trumpet blast, Joshua commanded the army, "Shout! For the Lord has given you the city!" Joshua 6:16*

Joshua had been given specific instructions on how to take the city of Jericho and the last thing that they were told to do was to shout. This was an act of faith for the giant walls of the city were still standing just prior to this and nothing had changed but as Israel faithfully followed God's commands, the city walls collapsed right in front of them. Sometimes we need to lift up a shout of praise and thanksgiving before we see the breakthrough, for God loves faith and without it, it's impossible to please Him.

## March 28

*"And I, because of what they have planned and done, am about to come and gather the people of all nations and languages, and they will come and see my glory." Isaiah 66:18*

One of the great purposes of God is to regather His people. The enemy loves to divide, separate and disperse but God's original plan has always been for families and nations to live in His presence on the earth. One of the primary goals of Jesus was to gather the lost sheep of Israel and after His death it was to bring others outside of Israel into the kingdom of God. This is why the disciples were sent into all the world to make disciples of all nations. Ask God to use you today to bring people to Christ and pray for the Jewish people to come back to Israel and see their true Messiah.

# March 29

Jesus replied, "They do not need to go away. You give them something to eat." "We have here only five loaves of bread and two fish," they answered. "Bring them here to me," he said. Matthew 14:16-18

Every year we take up a special offering at Passover in line with Deuteronomy 16:16 and every year we have witnessed miracles and multiplication as a result of our giving. We don't give to get, but we do know that God has promised to bless what we give to Him so we give joyfully and gladly. The disciples needed a great miracle and only had a little offering towards it, but Jesus was able to use it and so told them to bring it to Him. Whatever you have toward your need today, bring it in faith believing that Jesus will bless it, break it and supernaturally multiply it.

# March 30

"Go, consecrate the people...for this is what the Lord, the God of Israel, says: There are devoted things among you, Israel. You cannot stand against your enemies until you remove them." Joshua 7:13

Achan had taken spoils from the city of Jericho that belonged to God and had lied about it as well. His name means troubler and he literally brought trouble to the nation as a result of his actions so that they became powerless against the enemy. It was only when Joshua dealt with this sin that Israel was restored to God's favour and blessing again. We too are called to be holy and cannot afford to accommodate any sin in our lives but must confess it and turn from it in order to walk in fellowship with the Lord and be victorious against the enemy.

# March 31

> Then the Lord reached out his hand and touched my mouth and said to me, "I have put my words in your mouth. See, today I appoint you over nations and kingdoms to uproot and tear down, to destroy and overthrow, to build and to plant." Jeremiah 1:9-10

If only we knew how much power we had as the people of God and how much our prayers and words affect this world. Often we can pray and think that nothing is happening or changing when in fact there is great activity going on in the spiritual realms that we cannot see. Daniel had to intercede for his nation for twenty one days even though God answered Him on day one for it took that long to get through the spiritual realms. Don't stop praying for your loved ones, your area and your nation for your prayers are being heard by God and are changing people and places more than you realise.

# April 1

And the Lord said to Joshua...Take all the fighting men with you, and arise, go up to Ai. See, I have given into your hand the king of Ai, and his people, his city, and his land. Joshua 8:1

In the chapter before this, the army of Israel was defeated by the men of Ai because Achan had kept some of the plunder for himself when it belonged to God. Joshua dealt with Achan and his family and removed the nation from God's judgement. The Lord then gave them a second chance to conquer the enemy, which they took and prevailed. God is able to give you another chance today if you need it, for He is the God of the second chance. All we need to do is repent of any known sin and turn to Him again for his help and grace.

# April 2

Truly I tell you, if you have faith as small as a mustard seed, you can say to this mountain, 'Move from here to there,' and it will move. Nothing will be impossible for you. Matthew 17:21

Atoms are so small that a special microscope is needed to see them, yet they are a key component in the denotation of a nuclear bomb which can change the landscape of a country when activated. This is how faith works. We don't need to have the faith of a great saint of old; we just need enough to believe that God's word is true and that we can do what it says we can do. Ask Him for this kind of faith today that will change your life and the life of those around you.

## April 3

> And as they fled before Israel, while they were going down the ascent of Beth-horon, the Lord threw down large stones from heaven on them as far as Azekah, and they died. Joshua 10:11

As humans our natural instinct is to work things out by ourselves with our own minds, strengths and capabilities. This isn't necessarily wrong for God has endowed us with brains, bodies and resources in the world and expects us to use them. I've discovered though that so much more can be achieved in partnership with God. If we take the time to listen to His plan and strategy and ask Him to act on our behalf then we will always get to our destination quicker and overcome obstacles so much easier. Take a moment today to invite the Lord to come on board and take control of your day and watch what He can do.

## April 4

> "Again, truly I tell you that if two of you on earth agree about anything they ask for, it will be done for them by my Father in heaven. For where two or three gather in my name, there am I with them." Matthew 18:19

We can be tempted to think that Christ is only present in large, dynamic church gatherings when in fact He is as much present when a small cluster of believers come together to pray in His name. We don't need a fancy venue, high profile speakers or the latest technology to connect with heaven; just a few faithful friends who believe in God's word and can stand with us and agree with us in prayer. Ask God for one or two prayer partners today if you don't have any already and expect the Holy Spirit to be with you as you meet and pray.

## April 5

As the LORD commanded his servant Moses, so Moses commanded Joshua, and Joshua did it; he left nothing undone of all that the LORD commanded Moses. Joshua 11:15

It is important to do what God has called us to for the Bible tells us that obedience is better than sacrifice. In other words it's better to do the right thing the first time than to have to say sorry and repent for not being obedient. Before asking God for new steps to take, make sure you've completed the tasks He has already given to you to do. The end of something is always better than the beginning for it brings it to completion and we can have the satisfaction of knowing it's done. Jesus was faithful right to the end and was able to declare at the cross "it is finished!"

## April 6

Jesus looked at them and said, "With man this is impossible, but with God all things are possible." Matthew 19:26

As I write this our ministry is looking to step out into a new venture that is outside our normal comfort zone. It's both exciting and daunting but we know that if God has called us to it then He will open up the way and make it possible. You and I will continue to face seemingly impossible and challenging situations as we keep serving the Lord but it shouldn't faze us or intimate us. We know by experience and by the word that God is faithful and will not fail us in any circumstance we find ourselves in.

## April 7

*"This is the land that remains: all the regions of the Philistines and Geshurites, from the Shihor River on the east of Egypt to the territory of Ekron on the north...Gaza, Ashdod, Ashkelon, Gath and Ekron. Joshua 12:2-3*

Joshua and the nation of Israel had been very successful in taking over the land of Canaan as God instructed them to, yet at the same time, there were still large areas to be conquered. These regions would eventually be subdued later on especially by king David, but certain places became a stronghold for the enemy against Israel and even today we see the results of this as the Jewish people battle fierce opponents in Gaza and other places. Spiritually we need to uproot and destroy all sin in our lives as we are made aware of it so that it doesn't come back to harass and attack us and by God's grace we will.

## April 8

This is what the LORD says: "Stand at the crossroads and look; ask for the ancient paths, ask where the good way is, and walk in it, and you will find rest for your souls." Jeremiah 6:16

Everyday we are faced with the choice to go God's way or our own way. The old children's Sunday school song talks about both Jesus and Satan standing at the crossroads of life and each offering an alternative path. One leads to life and blessing and the other to death and destruction. There is nothing that the enemy can give us that will be beneficial to our souls, for he only comes to steal, kill and destroy but Jesus wants to give us abundant life that will last forever. Choose God's way today with the help of the Holy Spirit and you'll not regret it.

## April 9

*So here I am today, eighty-five years old! I am still as strong today as the day Moses sent me out; I'm just as vigorous to go out to battle now as I was then. Joshua 14:10-11*

Caleb seemed to have discovered the secret to anti-aging. Rather than grow old and decrepit, he maintained his strength and vigour into older age, much like Moses did till his death. We do not have to expect aches, pains and other age-related issues to be our portion as we grow older but can receive supernatural health and wellbeing as we walk with the Lord. Christ has made us alive and that should be reflected in our body, mind, soul and emotions. I pray today that you will experience fresh power and anointing that will give you the grace to do all that He has called you to do.

## April 10

*The country was brought under their control, but there were still seven Israelite tribes who had not yet received their inheritance. So Joshua said to the Israelites: "How long will you wait before you begin to take possession of the land that the LORD, the God of your ancestors, has given you? Joshua 18:1-3*

These seven tribes had got used to living a nomadic lifestyle without the need to fight for territory. They had become slack in possessing the land and as a result had not received the inheritance God had promised to them. Spiritual apathy is a dangerous trait that we must refuse to give in to. God has given us countless promises to inherit but we can only receive them when we fight the good fight of faith and wage a good warfare. Don't settle for less today but press on to take hold of that for which Christ took hold of you.

# April 11

> The LORD gave them rest on every side, just as he had sworn to their ancestors. Not one of their enemies withstood them; the LORD gave all their enemies into their hands. Not one of all the LORD's good promises to Israel failed; every one was fulfilled.
> Joshua 21:44-45

There are literally thousands of promises in the Bible for us to take hold of. Promises of salvation, deliverance, rescue, forgiveness, transformation, help, life, strength and so much more. The more we read God's word, the more we will discover what He has offered to us and the more we will be able to appropriate and receive His gifts by faith. Don't miss out on all that is available today, but commit to studying the Bible and applying these divine promises to your life like someone finding great treasure.

# April 12

> "Do not leave Jerusalem, but wait for the gift my Father promised, which you have heard me speak about. For John baptized with water, but in a few days you will be baptized with the Holy Spirit."
> Acts 1:4-5

Yesterday I pointed out that there are thousands of promises in the word of God for us to discover and receive as believers. The greatest of these is of course salvation through Jesus Christ. The next is the infilling or baptism of the Holy Spirit. For the Spirit of God helps us to stay connected to Jesus and to live like Him on the earth. It is the Holy Spirit who shows us how to live as believers and empowers us to do it. Seek the baptism of the Spirit today if you have never received it and I guarantee it will change your life.

## April 13

> When the day of Pentecost came, they were all together in one place...They broke bread in their homes and ate together with glad and sincere hearts. Acts 2:1, 46

Acts 2, which records the outpouring of the Holy Spirit at Pentecost, begins in a large house or upper room and ends with the early church meeting for fellowship in homes. We often think of church as a building or large venue but equally Jesus said that He is present when two or three are gathered in His name wherever they happen to be. God wants to fill our homes in these last days with His presence and glory, so why not make a space where you can meet with Him and invite others to join you for prayer and fellowship when you are not at church. After all, it all begins in the home.

## April 14

> Remember how I have allotted as an inheritance for your tribes all the land of the nations that remain—the nations I conquered—between the Jordan and the Mediterranean Sea in the west. The LORD your God himself will push them out for your sake. He will drive them out before you, and you will take possession of their land, as the LORD your God promised you. Joshua 23:4-5

God promised this portion of land to the nation of Israel and told them that He himself would clear the way for them to inherit it. Recently there has been great tension over this very area and yet it is clear from scripture that it belongs to the Jewish people. Pray for Israel to be free from war and conflict and to live in freedom and peace under God's protection and love and that the nations around her would bless her and not fight against her.

## April 15

But if serving the LORD seems undesirable to you, then choose for yourselves this day whom you will serve, whether the gods your ancestors served beyond the Euphrates, or the gods of the Amorites, in whose land you are living. But as for me and my household, we will serve the LORD. Joshua 24:15

Everyday we have the choice to follow the Lord or not. We can only give ourselves to God if we have firmly decided in our heart to do so and through the power of the Holy Spirit. He will give us the desire to want to please the Father and will lead us in paths of righteousness. If you make the right decisions today then it'll have a lasting effect on your family and those who follow you and you will leave behind a godly legacy.

## April 16

Day after day, in the temple courts and from house to house, they never stopped teaching and proclaiming the good news that Jesus is the Messiah. Acts 5:42

The good news is for everyone, all the time. I try to give out at least one gospel card to someone everyday if it's possible. Of course there will be days that I can't for some reason but I'm always conscious that people need to hear the gospel and there will be days that I give out more. When someone has been truly forgiven and set free they want to share it with others and not keep it to themselves. If someone found the cure for every sickness and disease then they would have to tell others and it's the same with the gospel for it's the only way to be saved.

## April 17

*"If you are willing, you can make me clean." ..."I am willing," he said. "Be clean!" Immediately the leprosy left him and he was cleansed. Mark 1:40-41*

We can sometimes fall into the trap of believing that God doesn't want to heal or deliver us; that we are not worthy enough or that we deserve what we are going through. The opposite is true for the Lord is full of mercy and unfailing love and is quick to respond to the needs and cries of His people. If we don't see an immediate answer it could be because the enemy is blocking His response like in the case of Daniel when an answer was sent forth from God right away, but the ruling spirit of Persia blocked the message for twenty one days. Remind yourself today that Christ is able and willing to help you and stay in prayer and faith until you see the breakthrough.

## April 18

*So he started out, and on his way he met an Ethiopian eunuch. Acts 8:28*

Tradition says that the first church in Ethiopia was founded by this high court official after he'd returned from Israel having met Philip. This spreading of the gospel took place because Philip had been obedient to the leading of God and was willing to go and speak wherever he was sent. As a result, another country on a different continent was able to hear the good news of Jesus Christ and be saved. Are you willing to be led by God today? Ask the Holy Spirit to lead and guide you to divine opportunities and be part of bringing in the great harvest souls in these last days.

## April 19

Do not be a terror to me; you are my refuge in the day of disaster. Let my persecutors be put to shame, but keep me from shame; let them be terrified, but keep me from terror. Bring on them the day of disaster; destroy them with double destruction. Jeremiah 17:17-18

We know that a great and terrible day is coming known as the Day of the Lord when God will bring ultimate judgement to the world for not believing in Him and instead rebelling against Him. We do not need to fear this time though for we have been promised eternal life through our faith in Jesus Christ and even leading up to this final cataclysmic event, anyone and everyone who calls on the name of the Lord will be saved. Pray for those around you today to come to a saving knowledge of Jesus before this takes place.

## April 20

All those who heard him were astonished and asked, "Isn't he the man who raised havoc in Jerusalem among those who call on this name? Acts 9:21

The early church was shocked when Saul suddenly became a follower of Jesus and some didn't believe it was true at first, for Saul had been one of the chief opponents against the faith up until that point. The fact is God can take anyone at any time and use them for His glory. There are many testimonies of people who were once steeped in sin, evil and crime and yet encountered God's love and forgiveness. This includes former terrorists, gang leaders, witches and drug dealers, for nothing is impossible with God. Sometimes the very people we think could never be saved are the ones that God takes hold of like He did with Paul.

## April 21

*"As I began to speak, the Holy Spirit came on them as he had come on us at the beginning...So if God gave them the same gift he gave us who believed in the Lord Jesus Christ, who was I to think that I could stand in God's way?" Acts 11:15-17*

Peter was so rooted in his Jewish tradition that God had to use a vision, an angel, a divine encounter and the word to show that Gentle believers were just as much part of the kingdom as Jewish believers were and in Christ they were all one. Sometimes we can get caught up in our traditions and ways of doing things and not see God's plan for the present, which might not fit our usual way of thinking. Let the Lord guide you into new ways of mission and outreach today that will help you reach out to people who you previously thought were unreachable.

## April 22

*Then, because so many people were coming and going that they did not even have a chance to eat, he said to them, "Come with me by yourselves to a quiet place and get some rest." Mark 6:31*

It's good to be busy and active for God's kingdom and to bear fruit for Him but it's also good to know when we need to get away and rest. While our spirits are immortal and not bound by time and space, our bodies are mortal and limited in what they can do and how long they can last. We must not be afraid to pull away from the demands of life every now and again in order to be refreshed and restored so that we can keep going and not crash. Even Jesus regularly sought to get away with the disciples whenever the crowds and ministry got too much for them.

## April 23

*Now in the church at Antioch there were prophets and teachers: Barnabas, Simeon called Niger, Lucius of Cyrene, Manaen (who had been brought up with Herod the tetrarch) and Saul. Acts 13:1*

Before Paul became an apostle and church planter he was known as a teacher in the church at Antioch. It's important to know your calling from God for we are all unique in how God has made us and we do not need to all follow the same route as everyone else. While it is good to aspire to the five-fold ministry of apostle, prophet, evangelist, pastor, and teacher, we should not become pigeonholed by other's expectations or societal norms. The Lord can use us in ways that are outside the box of traditional thinking and this has often been how He has used great men and women over the years in bringing awakening and revival. Stay open to the Holy Spirit today in how He wants to use you.

## April 24

*Once more Jesus put his hands on the man's eyes. Then his eyes were opened, his sight was restored, and he saw everything clearly. Mark 8:25*

When people come to faith in Jesus for the first time it is like they can suddenly see what was previously hidden to them. Suddenly they can see the sinful condition of their hearts and their great need for a Saviour. This is because Jesus is the Light of the World and when He comes into a person's life, the darkness begins to disappear and that person can see more clearly. If we continue to walk with the Lord and follow His word then we will stay in the light and the darkness will not be able to overcome us.

# April 25

> They stoned Paul and dragged him outside the city, thinking he was dead. But after the disciples had gathered around him, he got up and went back into the city. Acts 14:19-20

This story has always fascinated me for Paul was stoned by the unbelieving Jewish mob and left for dead but after the church had surrounded him, he simply got up and went back into the city. Some believe that he actually died and was raised back to life again and that it was during this time that he received the heavenly vision he talks about in 2 Corinthians 12. What is certain is that we serve a God of resurrection power who can deliver us from every evil attack and carry us safely through this life until we reach our heavenly destination as Paul himself testifies to in 2 Timothy 4:18.

# April 26

> Let the prophet who has a dream recount the dream, but let the one who has my word speak it faithfully..."Is not my word like fire," declares the LORD, "and like a hammer that breaks a rock in pieces? Jeremiah 23:28-29

In this chapter, God makes a distinction between true and false prophets. There were many voices that were prophesying peace and safety to the people while they were living in sin and rebellion against God and were about to be judged by Him. A true prophet or prophetic voice will speak the whole truth and not be afraid to confront and condemn what is wrong and ungodly. They will also speak from the unchanging word of God that has the same power as a fire or a hammer - to burn up the chaff of false teaching and break every lie and pretension that sets itself up against the knowledge of Jesus Christ.

## April 27

> Then a cloud appeared and covered them, and a voice came from the cloud: "This is my Son, whom I love. Listen to him!" Mark 9:7

If we want to know how to live right then we must follow and obey Jesus for He was sent by God to reveal the Fathers heart and to establish a new covenant of love through His blood and not through the law. There are many voices and teachings and ways in the world today, but there is only one way, one truth and one life and that is in the Son of God. Take time today to listen to the Lord and meditate on His word. Hebrews 1:2 says, "in these last days he has spoken to us by his Son, whom he appointed heir of all things, and through whom also he made the universe."

## April 28

> About midnight Paul and Silas were praying and singing hymns to God, and the other prisoners were listening to them. Suddenly there was such a violent earthquake that the foundations of the prison were shaken. At once all the prison doors flew open, and everyone's chains came loose. Acts 16:25-26

Praise always brings a breakthrough and will lead us into God's presence. When the Israelites travelled through the wilderness, the tribe of Judah led the way. Judah means praise and shows us that praise should always come first. Psalm 100:4 confirms this when it says, "Enter his gates with thanksgiving and his courts with praise; give thanks to him and praise his name." Keep praising Him today.

# April 29

*Then Manoah prayed to the LORD: "Pardon your servant, Lord. I beg you to let the man of God you sent to us come again to teach us how to bring up the boy who is to be born." Judges 13:8*

Manoah prayed a wise prayer here. He didn't just accept the promise of a special son who would be set apart, but he also prayed for the wisdom in knowing how to raise him. Often we can receive a vision or a promise for our life, but we don't know how to implement it and steward it. Solomon was given a great kingdom to rule, so he asked God for great wisdom to know how to manage it. Ask the Lord for strategy and guidance in how to handle what He has given you; whether it's a partner, a child, a job, a ministry or an opportunity. James 1:5 says, "If any of you lacks wisdom, you should ask God, who gives generously to all without finding fault, and it will be given to you." So go ahead and ask God today.

# April 30

*Even so, when you see these things happening, you know that it is near, right at the door." Mark 13:29*

There are many events taking place right now that all point to Christ's soon return. America had a solar eclipse on April 8 and won't see another one for around 20 years. The Jews are getting ready to sacrifice a red heifer to prepare the priests for temple service which would pave the way for a third temple very soon. Israel is getting closer to the Gog Magog war as tensions with Muslims are at an all time high and there is much more. The fact is we are right at the end of the age and must keep awake and watching for Jesus to return in power and glory!

## May 1

*As he approached Lehi, the Philistines came toward him shouting. The Spirit of the LORD came powerfully upon him. The ropes on his arms became like charred flax, and the bindings dropped from his hands. Judges 15:14*

Do you feel bound by something? An addiction, habit, stronghold or fear? There is only one way to be truly free and that is through the yoke-breaking anointing of the Holy Spirit. Jesus went around setting the captives free when He was on the earth and told the disciples that the Spirit would continue the ministry He had started. That means the same power that was in Jesus Christ two thousand years ago is still available to us on a daily basis in the third person of the Trinity. Open your heart to the Holy Spirit in a new way this month and let Him break off everything that has tried to bind you.

## May 2

*The assembly was in confusion: Some were shouting one thing, some another. Most of the people did not even know why they were there. Acts 19:32*

God is a God of order and not of disorder. When people follow Him and obey His commands it brings wisdom, life and blessing. When people stray from God's laws, it leads them into error and deception. This is why the majority of the world is in the valley of decision for as Ephesians 4:18 says, "They are darkened in their understanding and separated from the life of God because of the ignorance that is in them due to the hardening of their hearts." The only way we can release the truth to those around us is through the life-giving power of the gospel of Jesus Christ that brings light and salvation. Will you share it with someone today?

## May 3

However, I consider my life worth nothing to me; my only aim is to finish the race and complete the task the Lord Jesus has given me—the task of testifying to the good news of God's grace. Acts 20:24

Jesus told us that if we try to hold onto our lives then we would lose them, but if we let go of them for His sake then we would find them. There is nothing greater than giving ourselves over to the Lord for His kingdom purposes. I've found this to be true whenever I've given time to pray, fast, give or share the gospel. When I give up my time, desires, resources and reputation for God, there is always greater blessing as a result. Make a decision to look beyond your own needs today and look for a way to lift Jesus higher in how you live. You won't regret it.

## May 4

Only if the heavens above can be measured and the foundations of the earth below be searched out will I reject all the descendants of Israel because of all they have done," declares the LORD. Jeremiah 31:37

Jeremiah 30 - 31 are great chapters that promise prosperity and restoration to Israel after they have been disciplined for their sins. God makes it clear that although they will be punished and scattered, He will bring them back again to their land and establish them as a nation once more. With all that is going on right now in the Middle East, we know that the Lord will bring His chosen people through it and they will eventually embrace Jesus as their Messiah and Lord. We must keep praying for this to come quickly.

## May 5

*There was no one to rescue them because they lived a long way from Sidon and had no relationship with anyone else. The city was in a valley near Beth Rehob. Judges 18:28*

It is so important to be in relationship with other Christians in these last days. The enemy is always prowling around like a lion to devour isolated believers and we must be connected to God and connected to others. This is why it's vital to be in a church or fellowship, for together we are stronger and can look out for one another, but alone we are sitting ducks. Ask the Lord to lead you to the right people today and for at least one or two close friends or family members who you can call upon in times of trouble.

## May 6

*While Jeremiah was still confined in the courtyard of the guard, the word of the LORD came to him a second time: "This is what the LORD says...'Call to me and I will answer you and tell you great and unsearchable things you do not know.'" Jeremiah 33:1-3*

Even though Jeremiah was imprisoned for speaking God's word, he was still able to fellowship with God and receive fresh revelation. The Lord was inviting him to ask for insight that could only come from heaven and not from human understanding. God wants to reveal knowledge and wisdom to us today and invites us to look to Him for divine instruction. We need to see with a higher perspective in these uncertain and tumultuous times in order to know which way to go and what decisions to make. Call to Him today and expect to hear His voice.

## May 7

*In the morning, LORD, you hear my voice; in the morning I lay my requests before you and wait expectantly. Psalm 5:3*

There is nothing like getting up early to spend time with the Lord. It sets you up for the whole day and prepares you for all that you'll face later on. I know that if I miss this important opportunity, the day will be a struggle for me since there is a very real enemy seeking to trip me up. Make a fresh commitment today to give the beginning of the day to God in prayer and devotion and expect to feel His presence and peace in a new way as a result.

## May 8

*Whoever digs a hole and scoops it out falls into the pit they have made. The trouble they cause recoils on them; their violence comes down on their own heads. Psalm 7:15-16*

Never think that people get away with evil. Even if it seems like they have the upper hand and are prospering, the day will come when they will reap what they have sown and will have to give an account of their wickedness. This is true for people around us in our everyday lives as well as for nations and corporations. God will deal with all those who oppress His people and take advantage of the needy and the meek will inherit the earth. Keep doing what is right and trust Him to deliver you.

## May 9

*Then Naomi said, "Wait, my daughter, until you find out what happens. For the man will not rest until the matter is settled today."*
Ruth 3:18

After we have done all that is required on our part in a situation, we have to leave the rest to God. This is often difficult to do because we want to be in control of the process and timing of the answer, but what we really need to do is to wait on the Lord to act on our behalf. If we take matters into our own hands then we run the risk of birthing an Ishmael and causing unnecessary complications, but if we can give the issue to God and leave it with Him to act then we will sooner find peace and safety in the waiting. The Lord wants to work things out for us in His way and His timing so continue to trust Him today.


## May 10

*Whenever Hannah went up to the house of the LORD, her rival provoked her till she wept and would not eat.* 1 Samuel 1:7

This is an interesting story because in the very place that Hannah was harassed and tormented for being barren, God heard her prayer and brought about a miracle child for her. Not only that, but her son Samuel went to live and minister there as a young boy, becoming Israel's prophet and judge. This tells us that in the very area where you are experiencing difficulty and conflict, God is able to come through for you and provide a miracle. Hosea 2:15 confirms this when it says the Lord will restore the prosperity of Israel and "make the Valley of Achor a door of hope." God can turn your area of trouble into a place of blessing today as you pour out your heart to Him.

## May 11

"But I will rescue you on that day, declares the LORD; you will not be given into the hands of those you fear." Jeremiah 39:17

When Jeremiah had been cast into a cistern and left to sink in the mud, Ebed-Melek, an Ethiopian eunuch in the king's palace, went to his rescue and pulled him out to safety. As a result, this official was rewarded with his own life when the Babylonians invaded Jerusalem. It's so important to help others in their time of need for it will always come back to us when we need it most and there will be a reward. Jesus tells us that when we help and visit the sick, hungry, naked and imprisoned, we are actually doing it to Him and He will openly reward us in heaven. Look for someone today who you can bless.

## May 12

To those who by persistence in doing good seek glory, honor and immortality, he will give eternal life. Romans 2:7

The Christian life is a struggle and a fight and we should not give up pursuing victory in every area. Sometimes we can deal with a problem quickly and without much effort and other times it can take much longer and even years to overcome. It is through the struggle that we become stronger, more mature and more like Christ. We might be tempted at times to think we haven't achieved much, but when we look back at where we came from, we'll see how much we've grown and changed and come on. Make the decision to keep seeking the Lord and His kingdom to the end no matter what comes your way in life.

## May 13

*Come with me to Babylon, if you like, and I will look after you; but if you do not want to, then don't come. Look, the whole country lies before you; go wherever you please. Jeremiah 40:4*

Are you at a crossroads and wondering where to go next? Ask the Lord to lead you. Psalm 23:3 says "He guides me along the right paths for his name's sake." There are many paths before us but we can only take one. The Holy Spirit knows the best route to take and if we allow Him to direct us then He will. Sometimes a certain way might look appealing and right, but the Lord knows what will be best for us long term. Let Him lead you down the good path today.

## May 14

*The LORD came and stood there, calling as at the other times, "Samuel! Samuel!" Then Samuel said, "Speak, for your servant is listening." 1 Samuel 3:10*

God was trying to get Samuel's attention and it was only when Samuel gave the Lord permission to speak that the prophetic word was released. God is trying to communicate with us today and is calling our name but we have to be willing to sit down and listen and receive what He is trying to tell us. It's also interesting that Samuel was lying down when God spoke to Him for it suggests he was in a place of rest. We will hear the voice of the Holy Spirit more clearly when we shut out other distractions and noises and calmly wait upon Him.

## May 15

*Now the people of Beth Shemesh were harvesting their wheat in the valley, and when they looked up and saw the ark, they rejoiced at the sight. The cart came to the field of Joshua of Beth Shemesh, and there it stopped beside a large rock. 1 Samuel 6:13-14*

The glory had departed from Israel when the ark had been captured but now it had returned and the people rejoiced. Interestingly, it came back near to the time of Pentecost when the Holy Spirit was poured out on the early church and stopped in the field of Joshua which is another form of the name Jesus! When God's glory and presence fills our lives it will bring great rejoicing which is why David said, "restore to me the joy of your salvation" (Psalm 51:12).

## May 16

*Should you then seek great things for yourself? Do not seek them. For I will bring disaster on all people, declares the LORD, but wherever you go I will let you escape with your life. Jeremiah 45:5*

Beware of selfish ambition. This was part of the devil's fall from heaven since he wanted to be greater than God and was not content to fulfil the role and position that he had been assigned. The Bible tells us that if we humble ourselves before the Lord then He will lift us up at the right time and we don't need to take matters into our own hands. The more we seek to become like Him, the less we will want to promote ourselves and the quicker we will be used for His kingdom in ways we could have never expected. It's often in our weakness that He is most strong.

## May 17

*The Spirit of the LORD will come powerfully upon you, and you will prophesy with them; and you will be changed into a different person. Once these signs are fulfilled, do whatever your hand finds to do, for God is with you. 1 Samuel 10:6-7*

Nothing will change us like the Holy Spirit. We have led people to Christ and prayed for them and with them and have literally seen their physical countenance change as the Holy Spirit has filled them and begun to cleanse and renew them. If we try to change ourselves then it'll take a long time but with God's help, we can become a new creation in Christ Jesus quicker than by any other way. Ask Him to transform you today into the person that He wants you to be and believe that He will.

## May 18

*And we know that in all things God works for the good of those who love him, who have been called according to his purpose. Romans 8:28*

If you haven't already memorised this verse then now is the time to do it. I must have prayed, declared and confessed this verse more than any other verse in the Bible, for it covers everything that could happen to us and declares an ultimate good outcome no matter what it looks like in the present. God is actively working out all our troubles and issues for our good and His glory as we continue to look to Him and trust Him with the future. It might look bleak now but the sun will shine again and God's love and grace will fill you again.

## May 19

*The elders of Jabesh said to him, "Give us seven days so we can send messengers throughout Israel; if no one comes to rescue us, we will surrender to you." 1 Samuel 11:3*

Saul had just been anointed king over Israel by Samuel but had not yet established himself in the new role. Suddenly an opportunity arose to defend a part of Israel that was in trouble and Saul rose up to the challenge and cemented his position in winning a great victory. God will give us opportunities throughout our lives to serve Him and advance His kingdom and it is up to us to take hold of these God-given moments and not let them pass us by. Ephesians 5:15-16 says, "Be very careful, then, how you live—not as unwise but as wise, making the most of every opportunity, because the days are evil."

## May 20

*"Now then, stand still and see this great thing the LORD is about to do before your eyes! 1 Samuel 12:16*

It's not always easy to be still and wait before the Lord to move but still sometimes that is what we are called to do. We are naturally people of activity and purpose and feel that we must be doing something in order to be effective for the kingdom but there are also times when God calls us to wait and watch Him move in a situation. If you find yourself hemmed in today and you cannot go to the right or to the left, be still before the Lord and trust Him to open up a way that you hadn't even considered, just as He opened the Red Sea for Moses and the Israelites when they were cornered by Pharaoh and thought they were going to die. He is the great waymaker and will rescue you.

## May 21

> I do not want you to be ignorant of this mystery, brothers and sisters, so that you may not be conceited: Israel has experienced a hardening in part until the full number of the Gentiles has come in, and in this way all Israel will be saved. Romans 11:25-26

There will come a time when God turns His attention away from the church and back towards His original people and land. This is a mystery, for it seems impossible right now that Israel as a nation could collectively turn back to God and accept Jesus as their Messiah, but the Bible makes it quite clear that this is going to happen and is a prerequisite for Christ's return. Pray for the Jewish people today that this would happen sooner than later so that we can all be together in God's new and glorious kingdom.

## May 22

> Jonathan said to his young armour-bearer, "Come, let's go over to the outpost of those uncircumcised men. Perhaps the LORD will act on our behalf. Nothing can hinder the LORD from saving, whether by many or by few." 1 Samuel 14:6

Nothing should stop us from stepping out for God when He calls us to go. We don't need great riches, resources, people or qualifications but a willing heart that says "yes Lord send me, I'm available and ready." History shows us that God can do more with the little we give to Him than what we can do with much on our own. Just think of the five loaves and two fish and how it fed thousands of people or the three hundred men with Gideon who were able to rout hundreds of thousands of enemy soldiers from invading Israel. God only needs a remnant to work great miracles on the earth. Tell Him you're available today.

## May 23

Therefore, I urge you, brothers and sisters, in view of God's mercy, to offer your bodies as a living sacrifice, holy and pleasing to God—this is your true and proper worship. Romans 12:1

When we think of worship, we might think of standing in church or at home, lifting up our hands and singing slow, reflective songs with our eyes closed but this isn't the only kind of worship. The Bible tells us that our "true and proper worship "is when we continually offer our bodies and lives to God for His kingdom and pleasure. Our bodies were bought with a price and are not our own and as such belong to the Lord. God wants all of us including our physical bodies and not just our works or actions. This isn't always easy but with the help of the Holy Spirit we can achieve it.

## May 24

Rather, clothe yourselves with the Lord Jesus Christ, and do not think about how to gratify the desires of the flesh. Romans 13:14

In Revelation 16:15, Jesus warned us to stay awake and be fully clothed so that we would be unashamed at His sudden return. He is not referring so much to physical clothes here as He is to spiritual ones. The Bible talks about robes of righteousness and being clothed with Christ which means to have His mindset and Spirit in all we do. The closer we are walking with Him, the more we will be like Him and less like the world and we will not want to indulge the temptations that continually surround us. Keep looking to the Lord whatever situation you find yourself in and He will keep you in these last days before His return.

## May 25

*Whenever the spirit from God came on Saul, David would take up his lyre and play. Then relief would come to Saul; he would feel better, and the evil spirit would leave him. 1 Samuel 16:23*

Praise is one of our most powerful weapons as believers. We learn that it's good to enter God's presence with praise and thanksgiving in Psalm 100:4 and that we should praise continually in Psalm 34:1. King David knew about praise to God and it was one of the keys that kept him going especially in times of trouble. He was also from the tribe of Judah which actually means praise and which became the tribe from which Jesus Christ descended. Do you want to see Jesus in your life today and walk in greater victory then make a commitment to turn up the praise and keep it coming!

## May 26

*You are my hiding place; you will protect me from trouble and surround me with songs of deliverance. Psalm 32:7*

Yesterday we discovered the importance of continual praise before God. Today I want you to know that God is also singing over you. Sometimes people only see God as a stern judge or as a Father ready to discipline them, but the truth is He is singing songs of victory and freedom over His people just as a parent comforts a small child or baby with lullabies. The Lord is looking forward to the time when we will be with Him forever and see His face and in the meantime is singing over us with songs of deliverance until we reach that great day. He is cheering you on today so keep praising in return.

## May 27

David asked the men standing near him, "What will be done for the man who kills this Philistine and removes this disgrace from Israel? 1 Samuel 17:26

We have been taught to count the cost in stepping out to serve the Lord and rightly so for we cannot be ignorant about what we might go through for the kingdom in order to finish our race successfully. Equally we should also think about the reward that awaits us for giving our lives to God's purposes, for the Lord has promised to reward all those who seek Him and work in His service. Jesus told the disciples that they would be rewarded for prayer, fasting, giving, having to leave family or homes and even giving someone a cup of water. The apostle Paul looked forward to the crown of righteousness that awaited him and so can we as we continue to fight the good fight.

## May 28

The God of peace will soon crush Satan under your feet. Romans 16:20

Nothing conquers the enemy like peace. If we are at rest in the Lord and not anxious or stressed, it is much harder for the devil to trip us up or attack us. This is why he works so hard to pull us away from this position and why the author of Hebrews 12:14 tells us to "strive at peace with everyone." When our spirit, soul and mind is calm then we can hear God's voice more clearly and be ready for any ambush from the adversary, so take some time to get into this place today and remember the words of Jesus when He said: "Peace I leave with you; my peace I give you" (John 14:27).

## May 29

> Because of the LORD's great love we are not consumed, for his compassions never fail. They are new every morning; great is your faithfulness. Lamentations 3:22-23

Where would we be without the mercy and grace of God. No one is perfect and we all have times where we struggle to hit God's high mark for our lives, but He knows our frailty and is ready to pick us up when we fall if we are willing to turn back to Him. This doesn't give us a licence to sin and do what we want to do but an assurance that when we do come up short in an area then we have a heavenly Father who is ready to forgive us and restore if we are willing to repent and seek His face again. Don't stay in condemnation but tell Him you're sorry and embrace His compassion again.

## May 30

> Therefore you do not lack any spiritual gift as you eagerly wait for our Lord Jesus Christ to be revealed. He will also keep you firm to the end, so that you will be blameless on the day of our Lord Jesus Christ. God is faithful, who has called you into fellowship with his Son, Jesus Christ our Lord. 1 Corinthians 1:7-9

The Corinthian church had both strengths and weaknesses and Paul spent much of his letter dealing with the latter, but here he starts off by encouraging them that they are very gifted in spiritual gifts and are looking forward to Christ's return. He is also confident that despite their shortcomings, God is able to keep them from falling away entirely and will finish the great work He has started in them. This should give us hope today that God can also keep us to the end and finish what He has started in us.

# May 31

> You intended to harm me, but God intended it for good to accomplish what is now being done, the saving of many lives.
> Genesis 50:20

This is a statement we can boldly say to the enemy every time He tries to attack us, for God is able to take every misfortune and set back and use it as an occasion for His glory and redemption to be revealed. No one was hounded, persecuted and maligned like the apostle Paul, yet he too was able to say the same as Joseph and confidently declare in Romans 8:28 that "in all things God works for the good of those who love him, who have been called according to his purpose." Whatever is going on in your life today that you're looking for help in, believe that God can not only save you from it, but even use it to become a blessing to you and many others.

## June 1

*All those who were in distress or in debt or discontented gathered around him, and he became their commander. About four hundred men were with him.* 1 Samuel 22:2

David was on the run being hunted by Saul and yet God was preparing him to be the king and leader of Israel in the midst of his distress. As a result, men who were also discontent and bitter in soul for whatever reason gathered around David and became his loyal bodyguards. When we continue seeking the Lord and living for Him even in the middle of trials and difficulties it inspires others to do the same and as we find breakthrough and freedom so do they. Keep walking by faith for it will draw others to Jesus even when life doesn't make sense.

## June 2

*...while I was among the exiles by the Kebar River, the heavens were opened and I saw visions of God.* Ezekiel 1:1

Even while in captivity in a foreign land, God was able to speak to Ezekiel and commission him to be His spokesperson for the hour. We often imagine that if life is easier and all our troubles disappear then we will be in a better position to hear from God and start serving Him. However, it is often in times of crisis and difficulty that God's word and power comes through the most for we are in greater need of hearing His voice and seeing His face. This is why the apostle Paul said God was strong when he was weak for God's power is made perfect in our weakness. Don't wait for everything to be perfect before you seek God's will, but step out today no matter where you are or what your circumstances are and believe that you'll find Him.

## June 3

> Brothers and sisters, I could not address you as people who live by the Spirit but as people who are still worldly. 1 Corinthians 3:1

Paul talks about three types of people: the natural person who rejects the things of God, the spiritual person who walks by the Spirit and the carnal believer who although saved is dominated by the flesh. Christ wants us to continually live by the Spirit and not be mastered by fleshly desires which wage war against us. There is so much more of God and His kingdom to receive and experience but it is only found in walking close to Him, for it is a spiritual realm and not an earthly one. Decide today to put away anything that keeps you from God's best and keep abiding in His presence where you will find life and peace.

## June 4

> Hand this man over to Satan for the destruction of the flesh, so that his spirit may be saved on the day of the Lord. 1 Corinthians 5:5

As believers we are not meant to tolerate sin in the church. We are not responsible for those outside the church but we are to watch out for our brothers and sisters in Christ. Paul told the Corinthian church to excommunicate a man who was having a relationship with his step-mum so that he would come out of the protection and covering of the church and be led to repentance by receiving the consequences of his actions. God doesn't want anyone to perish but for all to turn away from sin and come to Him and He will receive them. Pray for those who are clearly going in a wrong direction today that God would convict them and bring them back to repentance and life.

## June 5

At the end of seven days the word of the LORD came to me: "Son of man, I have made you a watchman for the people of Israel; so hear the word I speak and give them warning from me. Ezekiel 3:16-17

God has called us to wait on Him, hear His voice and tell others what He is saying. We have a duty to share the revelation that God gives us with others to both warn and encourage them. I was only a teenager when God called me to be a prophetic voice for Him in the last days and it was in early 2020 when He opened the way for me to reach the nations with His word. If God has called you to speak for Him then walk in that appointed role and if He has spoken to you then share it - the church and the world needs to hear it!

## June 6

And that is what some of you were. But you were washed, you were sanctified, you were justified in the name of the Lord Jesus Christ and by the Spirit of our God. 1 Corinthians 6:11

The enemy will always try to remind us of our old life and past sins but we must instead remind him of our new standing in Christ and what He has done for us. Paul tells us that we have been washed by the blood of Jesus and made clean from all wrongdoing. The slate is now clean. We have also been sanctified and made holy - set apart by the Holy Spirit to live for God in a way that pleases Him. Finally we have been justified, which means we have been legally made righteous before God and can now boldly come before His throne of grace in our time of need without condemnation or fear. Praise the Lord!

## June 7

> But David said to Abishai, "Don't destroy him! Who can lay a hand on the LORD's anointed and be guiltless?...the LORD himself will strike him, or his time will come and he will die, or he will go into battle and perish. 1 Samuel 26:9-10

It is always best to let God fight our battles and defend us from people especially with those in the church. If we take matters into our own hands then it prevents God from working on our behalf. I've personally seen this firsthand when certain individuals have caused trouble for me. After giving the situation to Him and asking for His help, He has taken up my case and turned the situation around on more than one occasion. As Moses said to the Israelites, "The LORD will fight for you; you need only to be still" (Exodus 14:14).

## June 8

> I wish that all of you were as I am. But each of you has your own gift from God; one has this gift, another has that. 1 Corinthians 7:7

Paul was talking about marriage in this context and was telling the Corinthian church that it is a gift of God to be either single or married. He uses the same word for gift that he uses in 1 Corinthians 12 later on which talks about spiritual gifts such as healing and speaking in tongues. We need special grace from the Holy Spirit to remain single and celibate and to live with a family as a married person. Wherever you find yourself today, be encouraged that God has already equipped you and will give you the strength to remain in that place as long as is necessary.

## June 9

*No, I strike a blow to my body and make it my slave so that after I have preached to others, I myself will not be disqualified for the prize.* 1 Corinthians 9:27

It takes great skill and determination to climb a mountain and it takes the same focus and effort to come back down. You cannot afford to be complacent when descending from a great height. The same is true in serving the Lord. We can step out and do great things for God and see amazing results but it is important to watch our lives after having stepped out for that it often the time when we are most vulnerable and when the enemy would seek to take advantage of us. This is why Jesus told us to watch and pray so that we would always be on guard and not be open to temptation or attack.

## June 10

*When David and his men reached Ziklag, they found it destroyed by fire and their wives and sons and daughters taken captive.* 1 Samuel 30:3

Fire consumes and destroys like nothing else and sometimes God allows us to go through the fire to purify and refine us and burn away what isn't of Him. This is usually a painful experience but the good news is that God also promises to be with us in the fire and to bring us out of it into a better and larger place. When Daniel's friends were thrown in the fiery furnace in Babylon, they were not only unharmed but a fourth man was seen with them and that man was Jesus. Be encouraged that He will also be with you when you go through the fire or the waters and afterwards will enlarge your territory and lift you up!

## June 11

*These things happened to them as examples and were written down as warnings for us, on whom the culmination of the ages has come. 1 Corinthians 10:11-12*

Paul warns the church here to stay away from idolatry, sexual immorality, testing Christ and grumbling, for this is what the Israelites did in the wilderness and were punished for it and now they serve as examples and warnings for us. If you're going through some kind of temptation then remember that you're not alone and other believers are probably going through the same thing, but also remember that God can and will make a way of escape for you so that you can walk away from it and not give in. Ask Him to help you today.

## June 12

*Then one of the cherubim reached out his hand to the fire that was among them. He took up some of it and put it into the hands of the man in linen, who took it and went out. Ezekiel 10:7*

As believers we are all called to go out and be witnesses of Jesus and take the gospel to the world. We cannot do this in our own strength or ability but we need the Holy Spirit to fill us up and speak through us. Some refer to this as being "on fire" for the Lord. When we have the flame of the Spirit then our words and testimony become much more powerful making it easier to reach people. A famous preacher once said, "When you set yourself on fire, people love to come and see you burn." Get into the presence of the Lord today so that when you go out people will know you have been with Jesus.

## June 13

*Love never fails. But where there are prophecies, they will cease; where there are tongues, they will be stilled; where there is knowledge, it will pass away.* 1 Corinthians 13:8

Love is one of the few spiritual gifts that will continue in heaven for we will not need to prophesy, or speak in tongues, or perform miracles or healing, since we will be face to face with God and the imperfect will be perfected. This is why it is so important to walk in love now above all else for it shows we belong to God and are born of Him. People who have died and experienced heaven often say that one of things that stands out most there is the love that comes from God and from others and it usually makes them want to stay. At the end of the day, our greatest need is to love and be loved and this is only truly fulfilled in God through Jesus.

## June 14

*so David inquired of the LORD, and he answered, "Do not go straight up, but circle around behind them and attack them in front of the poplar trees."* 2 Samuel 5:23-24

We should always be seeking the Lord for His plan and strategy against our enemies. David had already seen a victory against the Philistines at Baal Perazim, but was wise enough not to presume that he would automatically defeat them again in the same way. It was worth it for God gave Him a different battle plan that ensured he would be victorious. We need to keep in fresh communion with the Lord to be able to see how He is moving in these times and not assume that it'll be like He did things in the past.

## June 15

*When they came to the threshing floor of Nakon, Uzzah reached out and took hold of the ark of God, because the oxen stumbled. 2 Samuel 6:6*

The threshing floor was where the farmer would separate the chaff from the full stalks of wheat. It was the last part of the harvest process and was usually on a hill or higher area so that the wind could help in the separation. It was a significant place in the Bible. It was here that Joseph mourned for his father, Ruth reached out to Boaz, Gideon put out a fleece, Uzzah was killed by God and where the destroying angel struck down many in Israel after David took a census. Spiritually we can experience God's threshing floor when He refines us, disciplines us, separates people from us and brings forth the best in us like gold refined in the fire.

## June 16

*And we all, who with unveiled faces contemplate the Lord's glory, are being transformed into his image with ever-increasing glory, which comes from the Lord, who is the Spirit. 2 Corinthians 3:18*

There is only one real way to find lasting change and it's not through self-help, counselling or will power, but through spending time in the presence of God. The law or old covenant cannot transform us but as we continue looking to Jesus with the help of the Holy Spirit then we will be changed from glory to glory. For we will eventually become whatever we continue to focus on the most. Make a decision today to spend time with the Lord and try to just meditate on the beauty of His countenance without rushing away. We will do this in eternity in heaven, so why not start practising now.

## June 17

All the trees of the forest will know that I the LORD bring down the tall tree and make the low tree grow tall. Ezekiel 17:24

Earlier this year I was praying for my nation when I suddenly saw a vision of a row of trees in a forest. There was a very large tree that overshadowed the others and darkened the area around it, but suddenly it was uprooted and removed and a smaller tree was planted in its place and the light was able to shine through as a result. Shortly after this the leader of the nation resigned and another person was elected in his place and it was like there was a sudden shift in the atmosphere. We went from consistent dark, cold, wet days to sunshine and an increase in the temperature and it was just as I had seen in my vision. We must remember that God is in control of the nations and raises up some and brings down others.

## June 18

Though outwardly we are wasting away, yet inwardly we are being renewed day by day. 2 Corinthians 4:16

At the time of writing this, my Nan is 94 years old and is still walking around and in good health. One of the reasons for this is because she is a woman of prayer and her spirit is strong. The Bible tells us that our latter years can be some of our best years because even though our bodies change as we get older, our spirits are being forever renewed and quickened in the Lord. The date palm tree in the Middle East is known to produce amazing fruit after many years of growth and is alluded to in Psalm 92:12,14 when it says "The righteous will flourish like a palm tree...They will still bear fruit in old age." Your best days are not behind you but still to come.

## June 19

*Repent! Turn away from all your offenses; then sin will not be your downfall. Rid yourselves of all the offenses you have committed, and get a new heart and a new spirit. Ezekiel 18:30-31*

Each new day presents us with a new opportunity to walk with God in holiness and to leave our old ways behind. His mercies are new every morning and we can receive fresh grace to become like Christ no matter what we've done in the past. First, we have to turn to Him and turn away from what displeases the Holy Spirit. Second, we should be diligent in confessing and removing any sin that we discover in our lives and finally we must walk in the power of the Spirit that will enable us to overcome every temptation.

## June 20

*Then David comforted his wife Bathsheba, and he went to her and made love to her. She gave birth to a son, and they named him Solomon. The LORD loved him; and because the LORD loved him, he sent word through Nathan the prophet to name him Jedidiah. 2 Samuel 12:24-25*

After David had sinned, God confronted him through Nathan the prophet and struck down the son who was born from David's affair. David then humbled himself, repented and fasted hoping to save the child and although he wasn't able, it did bring redemption into the situation and after David had got back up and worshipped, he had another child which God loved from the start and Bathsheba was also recognised as his wife for the first time. If David could be forgiven and accepted by God then so can we. We need to be willing to humble ourselves, confess any wrong and seek God's face again. Then He will hear from heaven and forgive and heal us.

# June 21

*Now he who supplies seed to the sower and bread for food will also supply and increase your store of seed and will enlarge the harvest of your righteousness.* 2 Corinthians 9:10

God promises to not only supply our needs but also to provide us with seed to sow for future harvests. Recently, I felt the Lord give me an exact amount to sow at Pentecost. I had already given a significant gift for Passover and so wasn't expecting to give another gift so soon but the amount seemed fixed in my mind. I planned to give it a bit later when the money had come in but on the eve of Pentecost itself someone put the exact amount directly into my bank account not knowing my plans and said that the Lord had told them to give it to me. I was then able to sow this supernatural seed right away in obedience to God. Trust Him to always provide both harvest and seed for He knows we need both.

# June 22

*Therefore, since we have these promises, dear friends, let us purify ourselves from everything that contaminates body and spirit, perfecting holiness out of reverence for God.* 2 Corinthians 7:1

God has promised to be our Heavenly Father and receive us as His children and our part is to be separate from the world and not go along with their thinking. This will lead us to turn away from the sins of the flesh such as lust, greed or lying and the sins of the spirit such as pride, self righteousness or hatred which can often be worse. We must then become complete and whole in pursuing godly behaviour on a regular basis. This may seem like a great challenge to achieve, but we can do it with the grace of God and the help of the Holy Spirit.

## June 23

*But David continued up the Mount of Olives, weeping as he went; his head was covered and he was barefoot. 2 Samuel 15:30*

It's amazing to think that Jesus followed the same steps here as David when He went to the garden of Gethsemane after the Last Supper. In fact there are many similarities between the two men. Both operated in the role of prophet, priest and king. Both were born in Bethlehem and were the beloved of God. Both were initially rejected by their family but later joined by their family members. Both destroyed the enemy of the people. Both were betrayed. Both were shepherds of the nation of Israel and both will rule over Israel in the new millennium. The main difference between them though is that David suffered for his sin while Jesus suffered and died for our sin. No wonder He is the King of Kings!

## June 24

*All this is from God, who reconciled us to himself through Christ and gave us the ministry of reconciliation. 2 Corinthians 5:18*

The gospel message can be summed up in one word - reconciliation. Because of sin, mankind was immediately estranged and cut off from God. Although efforts were made to reconnect with the Lord throughout the Old Testament times, it was only when Jesus died in our place and satisfied the wrath of God on our behalf that we were all able to be reunited with our eternal Heavenly Father and Creator. Come back to Him today if you have drifted away and then help others find their way back, as an ambassador of Christ.

## June 25

*Even when I am old and gray, do not forsake me, my God, till I declare your power to the next generation.* Psalm 71:18

One of our main goals in life should be to communicate the gospel to those who come after us and to tell it to our children and their generation. I'm so grateful for parents who not only made the decision to follow Jesus and to live their lives completely for Him, but passed this into us and showed us the benefits of a faith-filled life. We don't need to ram the good news down people's throats but instead love them and show them God's power and grace through our life and actions. Ask the Lord to help you pass your legacy of faith onto someone else today who needs to hear what God has done for you.

## June 26

*"Because you have clapped your hands...against the land of Israel, therefore I will stretch out my hand against you and give you as plunder to the nations."* Ezekiel 25:6-7

Earlier this year Iran made a direct and unprecedented attack on Israel with a barrage of missiles. Fortunately most of them were shot down before they could cause any damage but just over a month later the president and foreign minister of Iran both died in a helicopter crash coming back from Azerbaijan. The president was also known as "the Butcher of Tehran" for the tens of thousands of Iranians that he killed. God promises to bless those who bless Israel and curse those who curse Israel. There is no way around it - the Jews are God's people and we must continue to bless them and pray for them until Jesus comes again.

# June 27

*But he said to me, "My grace is sufficient for you, for my power is made perfect in weakness." 2 Corinthians 12:9*

Sometimes we pray to the Lord and He hears us and answers immediately to our cries for help. Other times, there can seem to be a delay which causes us to keep praying until we see a breakthrough. This is what happened to Paul. The terminology he uses suggests that he prayed continually to be free from his suffering but God's response was that His grace was sufficient in the midst of Paul's weakness and pain. It's not wrong to ask for God's help and deliverance in our trials but don't become despondent if you don't get an answer right away. Instead trust that God will give you the strength and grace to keep going despite it and will eventually turn it around for good.


# June 28

*Examine yourselves to see whether you are in the faith; test yourselves...And I trust that you will discover that we have not failed the test. 2 Corinthians 13:5-6*

Tests and examinations are a part of life. We undergo them from early on especially in school and college to find out what we know and what is really inside of us. If we are prepared and armed with the appropriate knowledge then we will pass and be awarded. The same is true in the Christian life. God will test us from time to time in order to find out if Christ is being formed in us. He doesn't test us to destroy us but so that we can mature and grow in the process and become stronger in our faith. May we be able to say with Job, "But he knows the way that I take; when he has tested me, I will come forth as gold." (Job 23:10).

# June 29

> The king summoned the Gibeonites and spoke to them. 2 Samuel 21:2

They say you should pick your battles and that is true but you need to make sure you pick the right ones. Saul was commanded by God to completely destroy the Amalekites for how they had treated Israel after leaving Egypt but he didn't carry this out and had the kingdom taken away as a result. He then later attacked the Gibeonites who God had promised to spare because of the covenant they made with Israel and it brought a three year famine on the nation during the time of David until justice had been meted out for them. Disobedience will always bring trouble while obedience to God's laws and commands will always bring blessing to our lives. Choose your battles wisely.

# June 30

> He reached down from on high and took hold of me; He drew me out of deep waters. He rescued me from my powerful enemy, from my foes, who were too strong for me. 2 Samuel 22:17-18

There are times when we feel powerless against the enemy that is coming against us and despite our prayers, confessions, worship and warfare, we cannot get the victory. This is when God shows Himself mighty on our behalf. As we humble ourselves before Him and cry out to Him for help, He hears us like a father hears their child in great distress and immediately comes to our rescue. Don't be afraid to call upon the Lord in your troubles; He knows that we are only human and He can rescue us unharmed from every battle waged against us if only we'll depend upon Him completely.

## July 1

*I have been crucified with Christ and I no longer live, but Christ lives in me. Galatians 2:20*

This is probably one of the most powerful verses in the Bible and should be memorised. I remember learning this verse as a young man seeking to please God and live for Him and I would confess it on a regular basis until I felt that I was being changed by it. It is a declaration of identification with Christ and what He has done for us at the cross. Sin and temptation can seem so powerful and irresistible at times but because of Jesus we have died to the flesh and the desires of the world and now have His power and grace within us to live a holy life by faith in Him. If you're struggling with something today, keep confessing this verse until you get the victory.

## July 2

*These are the last words of David. 2 Samuel 23:1*

A person's last words are important for they reveal the heart of the person and often the sum of that person's life. David lived his life for God and was even called a man after God's own heart so it wasn't surprising that his final address was anointed by the Holy Spirit and reflected his unwavering trust in the Lord. What will your last words be? If you want to have a great confession at the end then start working towards it now by faith. It's never too late to change and some have even turned to God in their final moments but we don't have to leave it that long and can open our hearts to Him today.

## July 3

*...he commanded our ancestors to teach their children, so the next generation would know them, even the children yet to be born.*
Psalm 78:5-6

I am so grateful for what has been passed down to me from my parents and grandparents and I'm now committed to passing on what I have been taught to my children. I'm also thankful for what Christian men and women have done for my nation over the centuries. As a result of their prayers, preaching, persecution and even death, the UK is now in the top ten countries for personal freedom. I'm eternally grateful for what Christ has done for me when He came from heaven to earth to take my place and redeem me from eternal death and destruction. This legacy is too great to keep to ourselves; we must pass it on to the next generation until they have experienced the goodness and mercy of God for themselves.

## July 4

*Christ redeemed us from the curse of the law by becoming a curse for us, for it is written: "Cursed is everyone who is hung on a pole."*
Galatians 3:13

We were once alienated from God and under the curse of sin but have now been set free through the precious blood of Jesus! The curse has been broken and we can now build a new legacy of righteousness for us and those who will come after us. The Bible promises that God will show His unfailing love to thousands of descendants of the person who loves Him and keeps His commandments. Know today that every curse against you is broken and instead God's blessing and unfailing love belongs to you.

## July 5

*And David shepherded them with integrity of heart; with skillful hands he led them.* Psalm 78:72

The New Testament tells us that it's a good thing to aspire to be a leader and gives us a description of the qualities required in 1 Timothy 3. David is also described as a model leader who ruled with integrity and skill. While the first of these attributes is sadly lacking among some leaders in the world today, it doesn't need to be the case in the church. With the help of the Holy Spirit we can have authentic and Christ-like shepherds of the flock again that are an example both to the church and the world and if you want to be one of them then ask God to prepare you for this today.

## July 6

*"As surely as the LORD lives, who has delivered me out of every trouble, I will surely carry out this very day what I swore to you by the LORD, the God of Israel."* 1 Kings 1:29

David was a man after God's heart but he still faced many difficulties and challenges and at times his own life was threatened. At the end of his life though he was able to testify that God had been faithful to deliver him from every trouble. You and I are not exempt from trials and tests and will inevitably go through them as we follow the Lord, but the good news is the same God who rescued David will also rescue us as we cry out to Him and look to Him as our Saviour, Redeemer and King. If you're in a situation today that is overwhelming, look to the Rock that is higher than us and believe that He will lift you up on it.

## July 7

It is for freedom that Christ has set us free. Stand firm, then, and do not let yourselves be burdened again by a yoke of slavery. Galatians 5:1

This is a very powerful and important chapter for Paul reminds the Galatian church that they were called to freedom in Christ and are no longer bound by the law. The way to walk in this is to be filled with the Holy Spirit so that we do not give in to the flesh. Then we will produce the fruit of the Spirit, most importantly love, and will not live as the world lives in hedonistic ways. If we try to justify ourselves by the law (dead works) then we will cut ourselves off from Christ and fall from grace. If you've fallen into this trap then repent and return to the presence of the Lord and come back to the freedom of the Spirit today.

## July 8

Therefore, as we have opportunity, let us do good to all people, especially to...the family of believers. Galatians 6:10

Everyday we have a choice whether to bless or curse, to help or hinder, to do good or not to others. Walking by the Holy Spirit will lead us to want to be a blessing to those around us - even our enemies. Jesus went around doing good to all the people because the Spirit of God was in Him and so He healed the sick, drove out demons and cleansed those with leprosy and other skin conditions. Because of sin and our fallen nature, our natural instinct might not be to help others - especially when there is nothing in it for us - but the closer we walk with God and the greater we become like Jesus, the more we will have a propensity to pass on the goodness and kindness of the Lord. Look out for someone you can help today.

## July 9

*Praise be to the God and Father of our Lord Jesus Christ, who has blessed us in the heavenly realms with every spiritual blessing in Christ. Ephesians 1:3*

If someone asks you how you are, you should respond that you are blessed for that is what the Bible tells us we are! Not only that but we are blessed with every spiritual blessing that heaven has to offer through Jesus. There is no limitation to God's blessing, but an endless supply and it is not earned through our own merit or good works but through the grace and mercy of Christ. You may have many earthly needs but the best resources and gifts are those that come from above and last forever. Make time for the Lord today and as you seek Him you may just find both spiritual and temporal blessings come your way as a result.

## July 10

*At Gibeon the LORD appeared to Solomon during the night in a dream, and God said, "Ask for whatever you want me to give you." 1 Kings 3:5*

Solomon's generous gift to God made a way for him to receive anything he wanted in return. He asked for wisdom and became the wisest person in the known world at that time. His gift to God released a permanent gift and talent from God. I have discovered over the years that as I give my best gift to the Lord joyfully and willingly by faith, it has often activated a new level of work, income, ministry or opportunity. I give to show my appreciation of all He has done but He also gives back in response to my obedience and trust. If you need a breakthrough in an area today then I would recommend giving a gift to the Lord.

# July 11

*So David went to Baal Perazim, and there he defeated them. He said, "As waters break out, the LORD has broken out against my enemies before me." 2 Samuel 5:20*

Just after David had become king of Israel, the Philistines came out to destroy him, but God was with him and he defeated the enemy. We are then introduced to the ancient title Baal Perazim which means 'Lord of the Breakthrough' because God had broken out like waters against the incoming army. It also has another meaning though which is 'the Lord who overwhelms.' The enemy had tried to overwhelm David just after his long-awaited coronation, but instead it was God who overwhelmed the Philistines and He will do this for you the next time the devil comes against you.

# July 12

*The LORD works out everything to its proper end— even the wicked for a day of disaster. Proverbs 16:4*

Although we live in a fallen and broken world, God is actively working to redeem and turn around all things for His glory. It might not seem like it when we hear of all that is taking place, but a day is coming when everything will be fully concluded and fulfilled as the Lord intended. I believe that things are beginning to fall into place as we approach this final day for both God's people and the world. Proverbs 16:4 confirms this and reminds us that everything will have "its proper end." Even today, God wants to tie up the loose ends in your life and fulfill His promises to you for as Psalm 138:8 says, "The LORD will work out his plans for my life."

## July 13

> In building the temple, only blocks dressed at the quarry were used, and no hammer, chisel or any other iron tool was heard at the temple site while it was being built. 1 Kings 6:7

The Bible describes believers as "living stones" who are being built into a spiritual house or temple of the Holy Spirit (1 Peter 2:5). It also tells us to look to the quarry from which we were dug and cut (Isaiah 51:1). I thank God that He prepares us in the secret place before He puts us in the public place. Don't despise your time in the quarry - in isolation, loneliness and pain - for that is where God is making you and shaping you before He permanently places you alongside others in His heavenly temple.

## July 14

> Now to him who is able to do immeasurably more than all we ask or imagine, according to his power that is at work within us, to him be glory in the church and in Christ Jesus throughout all generations, for ever and ever! Amen. Ephesians 3:20-21

We often pray and quote these verses but it's not until we see it with our own eyes that it becomes a living reality. This was my experience growing up. I wrote these words out and declared them regularly and then many years later, I saw it come to pass and continue to see God do things that I either didn't expect or certainly didn't deserve. He wants to do so much more for us than we are able to comprehend or conceive and I pray that you will begin to experience His "immeasurably more" in your own life from today if you haven't already.

## July 15

*So I prophesied as he commanded me, and breath entered them; they came to life and stood up on their feet—a vast army. Ezekiel 37:10*

Up until this point there were just lifeless bodies laying on the dry valley floor but when Ezekiel prophesied the breath of God into them, they suddenly came alive and became a great army ready for action. This is such a prophetic picture for the church today that without the Spirit of God coming upon the church and filling us afresh, we are just people without power and purpose. If we allow God to breathe new life into us though, we will be revived and ready to turn the world upside down for Him!

## July 16

*And pray in the Spirit on all occasions with all kinds of prayers and requests. Ephesians 6:18*

I remember taking my driving test many years ago as a young man and praying in tongues quietly as I navigated the road and traffic in front of me. About half way through the test, the examiner began to talk to me about his children and how he wanted to enrol them in the school I was at. Before we knew it we'd arrived back at the test centre and I was pleased to hear that I had passed my test! We can pray in every situation and circumstance, whether we are at work, home, school, the doctors, the shops or at church and we can expect God to not only hear us but answer us in great and mighty ways, so why not try it today.

## July 17

She said to the king, "The report I heard in my own country about your achievements and your wisdom is true. But I did not believe these things until I came and saw with my own eyes. Indeed, not even half was told me; in wisdom and wealth you have far exceeded the report I heard. 1 Kings 10:6-7

We must remember that what awaits us in eternity is greater than we can ever imagine. People who have gone to heaven and come back almost always say that they didn't want to leave but were given an opportunity to come back and help others believe. God made this world perfect at the beginning but our sin and rebellion corrupted and spoiled it and it's never been the same since. The good news is that God has promised to create a new heavens and a new earth for those who love Him and that is what you can look forward to receiving as your reward.

## July 18

For I know that through your prayers and God's provision of the Spirit of Jesus Christ what has happened to me will turn out for my deliverance. Philippians 1:1

The apostle Paul endured great suffering for the gospel in a way that most Christians won't experience and yet he was able to say that it would work in his favour at the end of the day. This should be a great encouragement to us that no matter what we are facing today it can be turned around for our good and even become a source of blessing and breakthrough. God is able to turn our mourning into dancing and our tears into joy through the prayers and faith of His people and the grace of the Lord Jesus Christ in our lives, amen!

## July 19

*He humbled himself by becoming obedient to death — even death on a cross! Therefore God exalted him to the highest place and gave him the name that is above every name, Philippians 2:8-9*

We all want to be honoured and promoted at some point in life but we must understand the process of getting there. In order to go up, we must first go down. Jesus came from the glory of heaven to earth and laid His majesty aside in order to serve us and obey the Father's plan. As a result, God lifted Him up to the highest place for all eternity and He will lift us up also when we humble ourselves before Him and faithfully follow and obey His word. The world fights and hustles to climb the ladder of success and recognition but we look to the Father in prayer and trust Him to reward us at the right time and He will.

## July 20

*The righteous will flourish like a palm tree, they will grow like a cedar of Lebanon; planted in the house of the LORD, they will flourish in the courts of our God. Psalm 92:12-13*

There is only one way to grow in God's kingdom and that is to be planted. This means joining a Spirit-filled church that preaches the true word of God and loves God's people. It also means staying rooted in the word of God. Jesus told us that He is the vine and we are the branches so the only way we can bear fruit is to stay connected to Him. When believers drift away from either Christ or the church they put themselves in a dangerous position and disconnect themselves from the source of their life and faith. If you find yourself here at any point, run back to the Lord and His people and get planted again. It'll be the best decision you make.

## July 21

*Not that I have already obtained all this, or have already arrived at my goal, but I press on to take hold of that for which Christ Jesus took hold of me.* Philippians 3:12

No matter how many victories and successes we achieve in this life we will still fall far short of God's high and perfect standard in Christ. That is why Paul said that he pressed on in his faith to the day when He would stand before the Lord and be made complete forever. We are also a work in progress and cannot sit back when things seem to be going well or go back to our old life when things are difficult, but we must be continually looking forward to the day when we will see Him as He is and be made like Him in His image. Make a decision today to keep pressing forward no matter how you feel or what you've done or not done. You will get there in the end.

## July 22

*And my God will meet all your needs according to the riches of his glory in Christ Jesus.* Philippians 4:19

We often quote this verse when praying for provision or financial help but we never include the verses just before it which talk about the gifts that the Philippian church sent to Paul. The best way to receive something is to give something in advance. I learnt this a number of years ago when I needed income and work and after sowing a small seed into the kingdom, a stream of work and revenue was released to me. We never lose out when we give to God or others in His name for we will always reap something after we have sown and we can never out give God. Tap into His abundant supply today by sowing a seed of faith to the Lord and watch what He will do.

## July 23

> Then the man brought me to the gate facing east, and I saw the glory of the God of Israel coming from the east. His voice was like the roar of rushing waters, and the land was radiant with his glory.
> Ezekiel 1-2

Our greatest desire and prayer is for the glory of the Lord to fill our churches, homes and communities for we know this is what revival looks like. To arrive here we need both intercession and consecration which takes effort, commitment and holiness but it is worth the sacrifice for there is nothing greater than being in the very presence of the Lord. My prayer today is that we would see a move of the Holy Spirit in our day that would transform many people who have yet to see the goodness of God.

## July 24

> He is the one we proclaim, admonishing and teaching everyone with all wisdom, so that we may present everyone fully mature in Christ. Colossians 1:28

This is the ultimate aim of the church: to help every believer grow up to full maturity in Christ Jesus and become like Him in every way. It is like continuing to take exams until we pass the test and this is why God gave us the five-fold ministry and spiritual gifts, so that it would equip us on this journey of growing up in Him. We cannot stop learning, changing, progressing and maturing until that final day when we will meet Jesus face to face and see Him as He is and become like Him. Keep going forward today with this goal in mind and you'll know you're on the right track.

## July 25

And having disarmed the powers and authorities, he made a public spectacle of them, triumphing over them by the cross. Colossians 2:15

When Jesus went to the cross, the devil thought that he had conquered Him, but in reality he himself was being defeated and put to shame. Not only that but Christ took away the power of the enemy at the cross and now the only weapons he has are lies and fear. This is why it's so important to be full of the word of God and the Holy Spirit for the deception of the evil one will not be able to reach us while we are walking with the Lord. See yourself as an overcomer today and the devil as the defeated foe that he is.

## July 26

Since, then, you have been raised with Christ, set your hearts on things above, where Christ is, seated at the right hand of God. Set your minds on things above, not on earthly things. Colossians 3:1-2

Spiritually, we have been saved and set apart and now have access into the very presence of God through Jesus Christ. Before this we were lost and completely cut off from God. We now have to make the daily choice to focus and set our minds on this new higher life and not stay earth-bound in our thinking. Our souls will be pulled by the things of this world while our spirits were made to be a co-heir with Christ in heavenly realms. This is why it's so important to start everyday with the Lord in His presence and studying His word for it will give us the best possible start to the day and set us up for living for Him and not the flesh. Why not try it today.

## July 27

*The children of your servants will live in your presence; their descendants will be established before you. Psalm 102:28*

There are great verses in the Bible to memorise and declare for those who have children and this is one of them. Remember, the Bible is a book of thousands of promises and we should make a note of them and confess them on a regular basis. We all want our children to grow up in the Lord and stay in Him and so we should pray for them, teach them and ask God to keep them all the days of their lives. We know that the enemy is always trying to poison the minds of children and the next generation, but God's grace is enough to cover, keep and carry them through it all and bring them safely to His kingdom in glory. Never stop praying for them.

## July 28

*Some time later the brook dried up because there had been no rain in the land. Then the word of the LORD came to him: "Go at once to Zarephath in the region of Sidon and stay there. I have directed a widow there to supply you with food." 1 Kings 17:7-9*

God is our constant source of provision and sustenance and has promised to provide for all our needs in Christ Jesus. Like with most things on the earth, He uses people and circumstances to fulfil His purposes and this includes finances. When I look back over the last ten years, I can see at least four different ways in which God has provided me with an income and there was always enough grace to be there until it was time to move on. If provision is drying up in your life today, ask the Holy Spirit to lead you to the next source of supply and He will be faithful to guide you.

## July 29

And Elijah said to Ahab, "Go, eat and drink, for there is the sound of a heavy rain." So Ahab went off to eat and drink, but Elijah climbed to the top of Carmel, bent down to the ground and put his face between his knees. 1 Kings 18:41-42

God had already given Elijah the prophetic word that it would rain and Elijah had then in turn passed it onto Ahab the king, but this didn't stop him from contending for the promise in prayer. You may have received a word from the Lord recently or many years ago and are waiting for it to come to pass. Don't wait passively just hoping it will happen one day but pursue the dream, calling or word that God has put in your heart and remind the Lord of His promise to you until you see it begin to come to pass.

## July 30

"And the name of the city from that time on will be: THE LORD IS THERE." Ezekiel 48:35

There are seven compound names for Yahweh and this is one of them: Jehovah Shammah - the Lord is present. There is nothing greater or higher than knowing that God is with us permanently and eternally and this is what will characterise the heavenly city and new Jerusalem. It's also comforting to know that God is with us today by the Holy Spirit and is an ever present help in times of trouble and we can call on Him at any time and He will hear us and come to our rescue.

## July 31

*So Elisha left him and went back. He took his yoke of oxen and slaughtered them. He burned the plowing equipment to cook the meat and gave it to the people, and they ate. Then he set out to follow Elijah and became his servant.* 1 Kings 19:21

The fact that Elisha had twelve yoke of oxen to till the ground tells us that he had a significantly large estate which he was willing to sacrifice to follow the call of God and serve Elijah. Jesus told his disciples that if they did not leave everything and follow Him then they could not be His disciples. He also warned them not to look back after they had put their hands to the plough, which paints the picture of them working as spiritual farmers. We too must be willing to forsake all in order to pursue the Lord and His kingdom and like Paul come to the place where we can say whatever was previously gain, we now consider it loss!

# August 1

*Then Daniel returned to his house and explained the matter to his friends Hananiah, Mishael and Azariah. Daniel 2:17*

Have you been given a negative report or have an issue looming over you? The first thing we must do is to stay in peace and then like Daniel we should find one or two other believers who we can pray with and give the whole situation to God. We've faced this on a number of occasions over the years and have learned to not panic or be overwhelmed by emotions, but to simply bring our request and need to the Lord in prayer, believing that before we call He will answer. He wants to help you today with whatever it is that you are facing in your life and remove every mountain of intimidation and trouble.

# August 2

*For the Lord himself will come down from heaven, with a loud command, with the voice of the archangel and with the trumpet call of God, and the dead in Christ will rise first. 1 Thessalonians 4:16*

There is always a sound when God appears. When He comes back for the church there will be a shout which is the same word that is used to command soldiers or rowers in a ship with urgency. There will also be a voice of one of the highest ranking angels and then there will be a trumpet blast which was often used to go into battle or gather workers from the field. This trumpet call will wrap up the end of the church age. The rapture will not be silent then but a sound will go out across the earth and those in Christ will hear and understand it. Learn to discern God's voice today as He wants to speak to us before this great and awesome event.

## August 3

*After that, we who are still alive and are left will be caught up together with them in the clouds to meet the Lord in the air. And so we will be with the Lord forever. Therefore encourage one another with these words.* 1 Thessalonians 4:17-18

Many believers dispute the timing of the rapture and are divided as to whether it will come before the last seven years of earth or after, but what no one can dispute is that the church will be caught up at some point and we will meet Jesus in the air! So the most important thing is to always be expectant and ready for this and also encouraged that this will be when death is swallowed up in victory and we will go from mortality to immortality and be with the Lord forevermore. Now that's good news.

## August 4

*Jehoshaphat replied to the king of Israel, "I am as you are, my people as your people, my horses as your horses." But Jehoshaphat also said to the king of Israel, "First seek the counsel of the LORD."* 1 Kings 22:4-5

Do you need to make a decision today? Are you at a crossroads in your life and need to know which way to go? Go to God and ask Him to show you the way to take. Too often we are led by our own ideas, intellect, experiences, or friends and family but the best answer we can receive comes from the Lord. The Holy Spirit is our counsellor and wants to steer us in the right direction. Proverbs 3:5-6 says, "Trust in the LORD with all your heart and lean not on your own understanding; in all your ways submit to him, and he will make your paths straight." Find out what God is saying today by opening His word and letting the Holy Spirit guide you.

## August 5

*Now, brothers and sisters, about times and dates we do not need to write to you, for you know very well that the day of the Lord will come like a thief in the night.* 1 Thessalonians 5:1-2

Paul was only with the Thessalonian church a short while but in that time he was able to instruct them about many aspects of God's kingdom including the return of the Lord. They knew man would have his day and rule the world for a short period of time but that God would also have His day and judge His enemies and rescue and redeem His chosen people culminating in Christ's return. This period of time is known as the Day of the Lord and it will come as a complete surprise to the world but not for us in the Lord for we will discern the times and season of His return and rejoice at His appearing. As things get darker be encouraged that He is nearer than ever.

## August 6

*May God himself, the God of peace, sanctify you through and through. May your whole spirit, soul and body be kept blameless at the coming of our Lord Jesus Christ.* 1 Thessalonians 5:23

We are called to be set apart in this life and to be different from the world and the only way we can do this is through God and in particular through the God of peace. When we are walking in the peace of God then we have victory over the enemy of our souls and we are able to abide and commune with Jesus. This is why Romans 16:20 promises, "The God of peace will soon crush Satan under your feet." Let God consecrate you and set you apart today by filling you with His peace that passes understanding and leads us into victory.

## August 7

*May the Lord direct your hearts into God's love and Christ's perseverance. 2 Thessalonians 3:5*

Here are two things we need today and everyday: love and perseverance. God's perfect love will drive out our fears and establish us as His children. It will bring an assurance of His salvation and presence in our lives so that we can share this with others. We also need a persevering spirit just as Jesus had in enduring the cross so that we might be saved. Let us not be led away from God's presence today, but directed and guided into His loving arms where we will receive fresh grace and strength to keep running our race.

## August 8

*One day Elisha went to Shunem. And a well-to-do woman was there, who urged him to stay for a meal. So whenever he came by, he stopped there to eat. 2 Kings 4:8*

Elisha was a type of Christ and performed similar miracles to what Jesus did including the raising of a child from the dead and the multiplication of food. When seen in this light we can see the importance of what the Shunamite woman did when she invited the prophet to eat and rest at her home, for in doing so she opened the way for a miracle in her own life. When we make space for Jesus in our busy lives and fellowship with Him, we too open ourselves to miracles, signs and wonders and will hear Him say, "ask of me and I'll give you the nations!"

# August 9

*Such things promote controversial speculations rather than advancing God's work—which is by faith.* 1 Timothy 1:4

There are certain subjects and topics that cause more division and strife than unity or encouragement in the church. I discovered this first hand when we started to explore particular teaching on our YouTube channel. The rapture of the church for instance can be very polarising even among respected Bible teachers and there are different schools of thought about it. I've come to realise that what is always important is walking in love, sharing the unchanging gospel of Jesus and promoting faith rather than speculation or hearsay. There is a place to address difficult conversations but our day to day lives should generally be full of prayer, praise, study and edifying and uplifting words that inspire God's people to keep seeking Him rather than engage in heated debate.


# August 10

*But Naaman...said, "I thought that he would...wave his hand over the spot and cure me of my leprosy.* 2 Kings 5:11

Naaman had a preconceived idea of how the Lord would heal him, especially given his high rank and position in life, so he was naturally upset and offended when God's solution was less prestigious than he had thought. We can also fall into the trap of thinking we know the solution to our problem before we have allowed God to answer our prayers in the way that He wants to. Remember He knows what is best for us and His ways are higher than our ways so we should not be surprised if He chooses to rescue us differently to how we imagined. The Father knows what we need and when we need it and so we can rest in this knowledge today.

## August 11

*For there is one God and one mediator between God and mankind, the man Christ Jesus, who gave himself as a ransom for all people.*
1 Timothy 2:5

The aim of the church here on earth is to bring people back to God through a saving faith in Jesus Christ. There is no other name under heaven by which we can be saved. He alone is the way, the truth and the life. Even if people have begun to seek God through another religion or method, they will eventually have to pass through the narrow gate of the Great Shepherd of our souls. There is only one Saviour, Redeemer and Lord and our role is to point as many people to Him as we possibly can through our prayers, words, witness and life. Ask God to use you to draw people to Him today even as you go about your daily activities and He will.

## August 12

*So I turned to the Lord God and pleaded with him in prayer and petition, in fasting, and in sackcloth and ashes.* Daniel 9:3

Have you had a prophecy or word of knowledge about your life or future but it hasn't come to pass? We must realise that with every promise there is a corresponding need to contend for what God had spoken. Remember that God answered Daniel's prayers as soon as he prayed, but a demonic entity prevented the answer from reaching Daniel for twenty one days. For some of us, we may have been waiting twenty one years but it's never too late for God and every promise He makes is yes and amen. So make a fresh commitment today to take hold of that for which Christ took hold of you and refuse to give up until what God has spoken has come to pass in your life and family.

## August 13

Then he continued, "Do not be afraid, Daniel. Since the first day that you set your mind to gain understanding and to humble yourself before your God, your words were heard. Daniel 10:12

God is so full of mercy that as soon as we begin to seek Him, He comes out to meet us no matter how far we have wandered off or how long we have been away. This is illustrated in the story of the Prodigal Son for as soon as the father saw his son heading home, he ran out to meet him along the way. He didn't wait for him to get home and then scold him but ran to where the son was and embraced him and welcomed him back to the family. Isaiah 65:24 tells us that even before we speak and make a request of the Lord, He hears and answers us so don't be afraid to come back to the presence of God today and to tell him what you need.

## August 14

...in later times some will abandon the faith and follow deceiving spirits and things taught by demons. 1 Timothy 4:1

A few years ago during the Covid pandemic, I dreamt that I was in a room with a TV and suddenly the word deception came on in capital letters. I knew that it was a warning that a demonic spirit of deception was about to be released into the world and possibly through the media and sure enough, lies and manipulation have multiplied greatly since then so that it's hard to know what is fact and fiction anymore. The only way that we can keep ourselves from this spirit is to stay in the word of God and in the faith. So make the decision to base your life on what the Bible says and not what the world says and you can be sure you'll stay in the truth and not be led astray.

## August 15

> Then he assigned an official to her case and said to him, "Give back everything that belonged to her, including all the income from her land from the day she left the country until now." 2 Kings 8:6

God specialises in restoration and redemption. No matter what has been lost, stolen, broken or destroyed, God is able to replace it, repair it or restore it. Whether it is a broken marriage, a sick body, a lost job or something else, there is nothing too hard for the Lord if we turn to Him and pray for His intervention. I remember a time when I lost some major things in my life all at once and I felt that all I had left was my life and so I figuratively put myself on the altar before Him. About a year later, God began to restore everything that had been taken away and He can do the same for you if you'll give your situation over to Him and trust Him.

## August 16

> Those who are wise will shine like the brightness of the heavens, and those who lead many to righteousness, like the stars for ever and ever. Daniel 12:3

We may be mocked, despised and rejected as followers of Jesus while here on the earth but our eternal destiny is glorious. The light of Christ will shine in us and through us forever and there will be no darkness. Even now God's light is in us and illuminates every dark place. We have people in our online global prayer group who radiate the Lord even before they have prayed or said anything because they carry His love. Don't hide God's glory but let others see it and be drawn to it so that they too can become like stars that shine forever.

## August 17

*But godliness with contentment is great gain. For we brought nothing into the world, and we can take nothing out of it. But if we have food and clothing, we will be content with that.* 1 Timothy 6:6-8

We are sometimes tempted to think that if we only had a certain possession then we would be happy; whether it's a different house, vehicle, partner, job or something else. The truth is that nothing material in this life can satisfy our souls. It may bring short term enjoyment but long term satisfaction is only found in God's presence and Paul discovered this secret. He said that he had learnt to be at peace whether he had an abundance or whether he was in lack. Ultimately, everything in this world will eventually pass way but God's Holy Spirit inside of us will remain and will lead us to true eternal riches in heaven.

## August 18

*He remained hidden with his nurse at the temple of the LORD for six years while Athaliah ruled the land.* 2 Kings 11:3

There will be times in our lives when God will hide us from the public eye and keep us in a place of obscurity for a season. Sometimes He will do this to protect us or it might be to prepare us for a greater assignment ahead, but He will always bring us out at the right time. I remember when the Holy Spirit clearly spoke to me and said "you're coming out now!" For shortly after that pivotal word, City Lights ministry was born. If you've been in hiding, prepare yourself now for the moment that God takes you out of His quiver and fires you into the great and mighty plan He has for you.

# August 19

*All Scripture is God-breathed and is useful for teaching, rebuking, correcting and training in righteousness. 2 Timothy 3:16*

The Bible isn't just a good book; it is God's own book. It was written by Him through godly men who allowed themselves to be channels of His Spirit. If you want to know how to survive the terrible times of the last days warned about at the beginning of this chapter, it is by clinging to the word of God and not letting go. For the Bible can not only teach us and equip us, but it will also transform us to become like Jesus in every way. Make a habit to read it and meditate on it daily so that it becomes the first point of reference whenever you need to make a decision or need an answer. This world will eventually wear out but God's word will endure forever.

# August 20

*After two days he will revive us; on the third day he will restore us, that we may live in his presence. Hosea 6:2*

Sorrow lasts for a night but joy comes in the morning. Remember that no matter what you have been going through or facing, it cannot last forever but will have to change as God comes to your rescue. He promises a day of deliverance, revival and restoration whether your suffering was your fault or not. As we turn to Him and acknowledge Him as our Great Redeemer then He will come to meet us as surely as the sun will rise. Declare that you are coming into that third day of resurrection power and restoration. He raised Jesus from the grave after three days and He can raise our mortal bodies also, amen.

## August 21

*The Lord will rescue me from every evil attack and will bring me safely to his heavenly kingdom. To him be glory for ever and ever. Amen. 2 Timothy 4:18*

Here is another great verse to memorise, for we will all face attacks in life in different ways and we all need to know that God is able and willing to save us on every occasion. We can often think that what we are going through will last indefinitely and that there is little hope of escaping the situation - especially if it has been going on for years - but the truth is every demonic assignment will come to an end and we will come out victorious in Jesus Christ. I can testify to this; the apostle Paul could definitely testify to this and so will you as you see the deliverance of the Lord in your life.

## August 22

*The scepter of the wicked will not remain over the land allotted to the righteous, for then the righteous might use their hands to do evil. Psalm 125:3*

When ungodly leaders rise to power we do not need to be afraid or alarmed for the earth is the Lord's and He raises up people and also removes people. Instead we should pray for them that they would turn to God and govern righteously and fairly for that is the only way they can be sure of a long and successful career. I've seen leaders come and go here in the UK for many years now and it will continue like that until Jesus comes to reign as King over the nations. When that takes place every earthly leader will bow down to Him and every kingdom will become part of His great and everlasting kingdom!

## August 23

*For the grace of God has appeared that...teaches us to say "No" to ungodliness and worldly passions, and to live self-controlled, upright and godly lives in this present age. Titus 2:11-12*

Grace is not a licence to sin as some might be tempted to think, but rather the power from God to live a godly and holy life. Grace will give us the desire to follow Jesus and to repent and renounce all other ungodly pursuits. As a young man, I used to say "grace is our companion on the road to perfection." For as Paul says in this passage, grace teaches us how to overcome the temptations of the flesh and instead how to walk right at all times. Receive this indwelling power today so that you can walk in a way that brings Him glory.

## August 24

*In the twelfth year of Ahaz king of Judah, Hoshea son of Elah became king of Israel in Samaria, and he reigned nine years. He did evil in the eyes of the LORD, but not like the kings of Israel who preceded him. 2 Kings 17:1-2*

Hoshea became the last king of Israel because of the nation's continual sin and rebellion. God had warned them over and over, but they had refused to listen and repent and so He had no choice but to give them into the hands of their enemies. There was a glimmer of hope for them though, for the name Hoshea means salvation and is the same as Joshua - which is the Hebrew version of the Greek name Jesus! God was prophetically saying that the very last king of Israel would be Jesus Christ, the Son of God and the Savior of the world and His kingdom would last forever. You and I are part of this kingdom today because we have put our trust in Him.

## August 25

But when the kindness and love of God our Saviour appeared, he saved us, not because of righteous things we had done, but because of his mercy. He saved us through the washing of rebirth and renewal by the Holy Spirit. Titus 3:4-5

The Bible makes it quite clear that we cannot save ourselves and that our own righteousness is like filthy rags; which is why Christ came and died for us even while we were still sinners. The gift of salvation is something we receive rather than something we earn and it is received by faith and not by good works, so that we cannot boast in our own efforts or goodness. The result of this is a transformed life by the power of the Holy Spirit and one which produces good fruit for eternity. Thank Him today for His salvation in your life.

## August 26

If you, LORD, kept a record of sins, Lord, who could stand? But with you there is forgiveness, so that we can, with reverence, serve you. Psalm 130:3-4

Do you ever have flashbacks from the past or are you ever reminded of something you did years ago which you have since repented of and turned away from? I do not believe these reminders are from God, for there are a number of references in the Bible that promise us forgiveness when we truly repent of wrong actions. We are also told that God blots out our mistakes and remembers them no more. The likely cause of these thoughts is the devil, so refuse to pay attention to them and instead remind him that you are forgiven, cleansed and accepted by God through the precious blood of Jesus Christ forever.

## August 27

Hezekiah received the letter from the messengers and read it. Then he went up to the temple of the LORD and spread it out before the LORD. And Hezekiah prayed to the LORD. 2 Kings 19:14-15

This was the second time that Hezekiah had been faced with a great threat and on both occasions, his first response was to go to the temple of God and seek Him. No wonder he was known as the most righteous king of Judah! This should also be our first response when we hear bad or threatening news - that we immediately seek God's word in the situation and not try to work things out by ourselves. Remember God knows what we are going to face and encounter and not only has He gone ahead of us, but He has already made a way for us and He has the answer we need, amen!

## August 28

You have loved righteousness and hated wickedness; therefore God, your God, has set you above your companions by anointing you with the oil of joy. Hebrews 1:9

The key to a joy-filled life is to continually walk with the Lord with an attitude of thanksgiving. The result will be genuine joy that the world cannot give. People might experience happiness based on favourable circumstances or temporary pleasure, but joy is lasting and comes from the throne room of God. It will also stand out for it only comes from God. You and I can have a continual supply of joy today to strengthen us for all that we have been called to do. No wonder the apostle Paul told us to keep rejoicing in the Lord at all times!

## August 29

"Go back and tell Hezekiah, the ruler of my people, 'This is what the LORD, the God of your father David, says: I have heard your prayer and seen your tears; I will heal you. 2 Kings 20:5

What a great promise given to Hezekiah: he wouldn't die but would be healed and have an extension of fifteen years on his life! Not only that but he would be able to return to the house of the Lord to worship Him and enjoy His presence. Praise God that we have the same promise given to us today in Christ Jesus that He will hear our prayers, heal us because of the cross and restore us to Himself. We can be confident to ask Him for this today because Jesus made a way for us to enter the Holy of Holies and ask for help in time of need. So go ahead and ask!

## August 30

We must pay the most careful attention, therefore, to what we have heard, so that we do not drift away. Hebrews 2:1

If we want to grow in our faith and overcome every challenge and obstacle then we must do the following: read and study the word of God daily, keep meeting with other believers, stay in prayer and keep Jesus as the focus of our lives. We have to actively do these things to keep our walk with the Lord alive and steadfast. Those who drift and fall away don't always do it because of great sin, but because they simply stop investing in their spiritual life and get caught up and carried away by the things of this life and world and then one day realise they have lost sight of Jesus and are lost at sea. If that is you then there is still hope; call to the Lord for help and set your face to seek Him with all your heart today and He will bring you back to Himself.

# August 31

*Therefore, holy brothers and sisters, who share in the heavenly calling, fix your thoughts on Jesus. Hebrews 3:1*

Studies have shown that the human brain can have up to 60,000 thoughts with nearly 90% repetitive thoughts from the day before. This means that our minds are like trains that go in a certain direction most of the time and can be programmed to think certain things. The author of Hebrews encouraged the church to fix its thoughts on Jesus, for one day we will be with the Lord for eternity and so it makes sense to start directing our conscious mind towards Him now. There is nothing in this world that will bring the peace that comes from meditating on Jesus. As the old hymn says, "Turn your eyes upon Jesus, look full in his wonderful face, and the things of earth will grow strangely dim, in the light of his glory and grace."

# September 1

*How precious to me are your thoughts, God! How vast is the sum of them! Psalm 139:17*

Yesterday we discovered that the human mind can have up to 60,000 in one day. Here in this Psalm it is revealed that God's thoughts are countless and more than the grains of sand by the sea. What is even more incredible and life changing is knowing that the bulk of these thoughts are about you and I, His people! It now makes sense to keep thinking about Him for He keeps thinking about us and His thoughts are good. He is not planning our downfall or destruction, but how to bless us, redeem us, rescue us and save us. Whether we are awake or asleep, rest assured that the Lord is both watching over us and thinking precious thoughts about us all the time.

# September 2

*Let us then approach God's throne of grace with confidence, so that we may receive mercy and find grace to help us in our time of need. Hebrews 4:16*

It is important to know and understand that God is ready to help us and not to condemn us. Before we were saved we were by nature objects of God's wrath, but because of His great love for us, He made us alive in Christ Jesus and raised us up into heavenly places with Him. We now have access into the most exclusive place - the throne room of God and we can ask the Lord for help in any and every situation we face. So do not shy away today but come boldly to your heavenly Father for all that you need and you will find grace is waiting to be given to you.

## September 3

*We have this hope as an anchor for the soul, firm and secure. It enters the inner sanctuary behind the curtain, where our forerunner, Jesus, has entered on our behalf.* Hebrews 6:19-20

Hope is being able to trust in God when life is full of storms and uncertainties and we cannot see the way forward. It is being secure in His word even if forces are trying to pull us away or shipwreck us in some way and our greatest hope is of course in Jesus Christ. He has gone before us into heaven and prepared a place for us to be with Him and we have the assurance that He will not leave us here in our problems and battles but will deliver us from them all and take us to be with Him forever. There is surely no greater hope than knowing that we are His precious children and that He will come back for us.

## September 4

*Therefore He is able to save completely those who come to God through Him, because He always lives to intercede for them.* Hebrews 7:25

Never give up praying for your loved ones to come to Jesus. It may take years but God will hear your prayers. My mother came from an unsaved family but committed to praying for them and other relatives everyday and after a few years, one by one they began to give their hearts to the Lord. Jesus is continually praying for us in heaven and for those who will surrender to His Lordship for He knows who are His. A famous evangelist prayed for one hundred friends everyday during his life and saw ninety seven of them come to faith. At his funeral, the remaining three gave their lives to Christ. Don't stop praying!

## September 5

*He fulfills the desires of those who fear Him; He hears their cry and saves them. Psalm 145:19*

The Lord knows the desires of our hearts for it is likely that He put them there in the first place. I remember a time when I really wanted to be used by God and I kept praying for an opportunity. Eventually God fulfilled it and it brought satisfaction to my soul. Proverbs 13:12 says "Hope deferred makes the heart sick, but a longing fulfilled is a tree of life." I believe the key to fulfilled desires and dreams is to keep praising God even when it is not happening, for it will show God that He means more to you than what you want Him to do. Psalm 37:4 confirms this when it says, "Take delight in the LORD, and he will give you the desires of your heart."

## September 6

*Jabez cried out to the God of Israel, "Oh, that you would bless me and enlarge my territory! Let your hand be with me, and keep me from harm so that I will be free from pain." And God granted his request. 1 Chronicles 4:10*

The short story of Jabez stands out in the book of Chronicles as a great example for us. For despite a difficult and painful start in life, Jabez sought the Lord diligently, not just for himself but also for others. Commentators believe that he asked God to bless him so that he could free from harm, advance God's kingdom in Israel and raise up a generation of young people who would also follow Yahweh. We are then told that God answered His prayer. Don't be afraid to ask for what you need both for yourself and for those around you as you pursue the Lord's kingdom today.

## September 7

*So Christ was sacrificed once to take away the sins of many; and he will appear a second time, not to bear sin, but to bring salvation to those who are waiting for him. Hebrews 9:28*

Jesus came to the earth two thousand years ago with an express purpose - to die on the cross for our sins and to redeem all humanity back to God. We know that those who believe in Him and call on His name will be saved and this is what we proclaim to the lost. We also know that Jesus is coming back again very soon, not to forgive sin like before, but to bring the fulfilment of salvation to all those who have believed in Him. This is our hope and why we urgently need to tell others about the reason for His first coming so that they don't miss out on His return.

## September 8

*But we do not belong to those who shrink back and are destroyed, but to those who have faith and are saved. Hebrews 10:39*

The Christian life is not one of retreat or surrender but it is a life of pilgrimage and overcoming every obstacle that stands in our way. We are going up and not down, forward and not back. There might be times when the resistance is so great that we cannot advance but this is when we need to stand our ground and hold onto what we have already won. Then after we have suffered a little while, God will come to our rescue and strengthen us and give us the grace and power we need to get back in the race and back in the fight. Let this be your prayer today especially if you are facing opposition and watch what God will do for you.

## September 9

*And without faith it is impossible to please God, because anyone who comes to him must believe that he exists and that he rewards those who earnestly seek him. Hebrews 11:6*

As followers of Christ we must believe two fundamental truths: that God exists and is on the throne and that we will be rewarded according to our life and conduct. Sometimes we forget that the kingdom of God is based on a reward system and that everything we do will be judged for its motivation and merit. There are rewards for prayer, fasting, giving, serving, standing in hard times and so much more. Jesus encouraged the church by reminding them that He is coming soon and is bringing a reward with Him. When we live with this in mind it should spur us on to make the right choices and to keep seeking God as the greatest priority since He Himself is our greatest reward.

## September 10

*And let us run with perseverance the race marked out for us, fixing our eyes on Jesus. Hebrews 12:2*

The Bible calls us to run in the faith but sometimes we find it difficult to even move. This could be a result of spiritual warfare, exhaustion, discouragement, or a host of other factors. We don't have to stay static and stuck though for Isaiah the prophet promised that those who would wait on God would renew their strength and would be able to rise up and start running again. I don't know what has knocked you down or held you back, but I pray today that it will lift off you and you will be set free to run your race with perseverance and endurance right to the finish line in Jesus' name amen.

## September 11

*The ark of God remained with the family of Obed-Edom in his house for three months, and the LORD blessed his household and everything he had. 1 Chronicles 13:14*

Our lives will not stay the same if we are willing to host the presence of God in our homes. God is looking for somewhere to dwell here on the earth by the Holy Spirit and we are the temple that He wants to live in. We never lose out when we make the Lord a priority in our daily life but instead will open ourselves to blessing from heaven, on us and those around us. Most revivals have been borne out of someone willing to let God inhabit them - body, soul and mind. Make a decision to be the kind of person today who will make room for the King to stay.

## September 12

*If any of you lacks wisdom, you should ask God, who gives generously to all without finding fault. James 1:5*

God's wisdom is different from the world's wisdom. It comes from the author and creator of life and is not based on human reasoning and experience. If you had a problem with a product then you would naturally go to someone who knew how it was made and not to someone with limited knowledge. God is the only one who truly understands the human heart and how we operate and we should be quick to run to Him for help, advice and direction all day and everyday before we run to people. The Psalmist confirms this in saying, "Do not put your trust in princes, in human beings, who cannot save…Blessed are those whose help is the God of Jacob." Psalm 146:3,5.

## September 13

So David and the elders of Israel and the commanders of units of a thousand went to bring up the ark of the covenant of the LORD from the house of Obed-Edom, with rejoicing. 1 Chronicles 15:25

You will be amazed at who God brings into your life when you decide to spend time with Him and seek His presence. People are drawn to Christ in us even if they don't know why. I was a volunteer and attendee at revival meetings in London as a young man and one evening a famous TV presenter came to see what was going on and asked to interview me about faith and God and I was able to share my testimony with her. Others in the past have approached me saying there was something different about me and I've been able to say why. The more of the Holy Spirit we have in us, the more people will be drawn to the Lord through us.

## September 14

"In that day I will restore David's fallen shelter — I will repair its broken walls and restore its ruins — and will rebuild it as it used to be. Amos 9:11

We all have spiritual walls in our lives and families that represent boundaries, principles, morals and right choices. We need these walls to protect our hearts from the enemy and to walk in God's protection and grace. Sometimes these walls can get attacked and even knocked down in places and we find parts of our lives open and vulnerable or even in pieces. The good news is that even if this has happened God can rebuild and restore our walls and bring us back to a place of safety, blessing and protection. Whether it's a broken relationship, illness, or job loss that you've encountered, God can repair it today as you let Him help you.

## September 15

*He got into one of the boats, the one belonging to Simon, and asked him to put out a little from shore. Then he sat down and taught the people from the boat. Luke 5:3*

Jesus used a boat to reach people and teach them and today He is looking for people that He can use and work through in order to reach other people. We can make ourselves available to Him as we spend time in His presence and then obey Him when He prompts us to step out in faith. Peter gave up his boat for Jesus and it resulted in an overwhelming catch of fish after a long hard night of catching nothing. When we make ourselves available for Jesus to use then it will not only benefit us but will be a blessing to many others as well.

## September 16

*Or do you think Scripture says without reason that he jealously longs for the spirit he has caused to dwell in us? But he gives us more grace. James 4:5*

God is jealous for our company and time. He wants our spirits to connect and abide with His Holy Spirit so that we can stay in friendship and fellowship with Him. The way to achieve this is through His great grace. For it is by grace that we are saved and not by works. His grace is His mighty power at work in us in the midst of all our challenges and difficulties. Do not look at your own strength and abilities as you seek to please the Lord today but look to His matchless and amazing love that saved us while we were still sinners and then we will rest in Christ's finished work at the cross and not in our own futile efforts.

## September 17

> But Jonah ran away from the LORD and headed for Tarshish.
> Jonah 1:3

What is your Tarshish? We all have one at some point in our lives when we go our own way instead of God's way. The thing we need to know about Tarshish is that there is no place for us there as God's people and we will never fully arrive there. If we did arrive it would not be comfortable or blessed for we have a greater calling that we cannot run away from but must press on towards. I thank God that I wasn't able to live and dwell in my Tarshish comfortably but was led back home by God's grace into the wonderful plans He always had for me. Don't let temptation, fear or disobedience keep you from pursuing God's destination today for it's the only place where we are meant to be.

## September 18

> ...David took a great quantity of bronze, which Solomon used to make the bronze Sea, the pillars and various bronze articles. 1 Chronicles 18:8

David's victory over the enemy rewarded him with resources for the next generation to meet with God, for the bronze that he captured was later used by Solomon, his son, in building the temple. When we overcome the enemy in our lives, we make a way not just for ourselves but also for those coming after us. A parent who succeeds financially is able to provide for their children materially and likewise a believer who breaks through spiritually is able to help others advance in the kingdom. Let's be those who take back what the enemy has stolen in our lives and who are able to equip and empower the next generation for Jesus as a result.

## September 19

*The prayer of a righteous person is powerful and effective. James 5:16*

Our qualification for successful prayers is righteousness which comes from God and not from us. 2 Corinthians 5:21 says, "God made him who had no sin to be sin for us, so that in him we might become the righteousness of God." We are only made righteous through the precious blood of Jesus and not through our own efforts or works. When we believe this truth and walk in His finished work we can boldly approach the throne of grace and ask for anything in His name, knowing that He hears us and will answer us.

## September 20

*He said, "Young man, I say to you, get up!" The dead man sat up and began to talk, and Jesus gave him back to his mother. Luke 7:14-15*

Do you have a prodigal child today who started off as a believer but is now living a different life away from the Lord? Do not despair but commit to praying them back into the kingdom. I was once that young man who had grown up in the presence and promises of God but then I hit a short period of time where I was pulled in another direction away from Him. My mother continued praying for me and it wasn't long before I was back home and seeking to follow Jesus again. No matter how long it takes, do not give up contending for the salvation of your children. Hebrews 11:35 says "Women received back their dead, raised to life again" and so can you if you will continue to believe and declare God's word over them.

## September 21

*For you know that it was not with perishable things such as silver or gold that you were redeemed...but with the precious blood of Christ, a lamb without blemish or defect. 1 Peter 1:18*

The blood of Jesus has not only saved us but has opened us up to a brand new way of living that is full of purpose, meaning and opportunity. Although I was saved at a very young age, I later tried to go my own way for a short period of time and it was cold, lonely and empty. I realised that real life is only found in Jesus and anything else will not last. If you have found meaning in Christ then make it your goal to help someone else discover this truth and escape from a lost eternity today.

## September 22

*But the seed on good soil stands for those with a noble and good heart, who hear the word, retain it, and by persevering produce a crop. Luke 8:15*

After reading this passage, I felt motivated to try and share the gospel with at least four people a day and although it is not always possible, it is still something I try to aim for. In this parable, Jesus talks about four different types of soils that the word falls on but only one of them produces a lasting harvest. We must always pray that our words and witness about Jesus go into good soil that is fertile, soft and ready to take seed so that we can see fruit from our labours. Even if one person is affected by what we say or pray with them, that one person could end up changing the world for Christ so keep on sowing!

## September 23

*Always be prepared to give an answer to everyone who asks you to give the reason for the hope that you have. But do this with gentleness and respect. 1 Peter 3:15*

This is a great foundational verse for sharing the gospel with others, for it sums up the approach we should take with unbelievers - to be ready to share our testimony in a friendly and courteous way. Can you summarise it in less than thirty seconds? Sometimes we don't even have this long to say something about Jesus to people in passing, but just a few words in a few seconds can sow a powerful seed that grows into a mighty harvest. Don't be afraid to speak up for the Lord today for you just don't know who you could be reaching with the good news.

## September 24

*The end of all things is near. Therefore be alert and of sober mind so that you may pray. 1 Peter 4:7*

When we think of the word sober we immediately think of not being intoxicated with alcohol. For instance, yesterday I read about someone who had been struggling with drinking for a while, until a pastor prayed for them and they have been sober ever since! The Greek word for sober here though is more than that for it is talking about being moderate and temperate and disciplined so that we are in control of our bodies and minds in order to be prayerful and watchful at all times. This means that we should resist anything that blurs or diminishes our thinking and emotions so that we can stay in tune with God and alert enough to pray. If there is anything that stops you from being sober minded or temperate, ask the Holy Spirit to help you overcome it today in Jesus' name.

## September 25

*And the God of all grace, who called you to his eternal glory in Christ, after you have suffered a little while, will himself restore you and make you strong, firm and steadfast. 1 Peter 5:10*

We are not exempt from suffering; in fact the more we pursue the Lord and His purposes the more we are likely to face opposition from the enemy. God does promise that it will not last forever though and that He will rescue and deliver us from our adversaries. Not only will He bring us through our trials but He will make us stronger and more established in our faith than before. He will do this through His great grace poured out on us in Christ Jesus. So the next time you go through a test, remember that it will not last and that you will be in a better place at the end of it.

## September 26

*In the last days the mountain of the LORD's temple will be established...and peoples will stream to it. Micah 4:1*

It's comforting to know the final outcome of this world and of God's Holy Land. Despite Israel being under attack on multiple fronts right now, a day is coming when it will rule as the superpower of the world under the leadership of Jesus. Then the nations will come to it for knowledge, understanding, justice and peace. The Babylonian system of the world which we are now currently in will be destroyed forever and we too will reign with the Lord in the new millennium. Whenever things look hopeless and dark, just remember that we are not of this world but are looking forward to another kingdom yet to come and it will not be long till we are there.

## September 27

*'For three years now I've been coming to look for fruit on this fig tree and haven't found any. Cut it down! Why should it use up the soil?' Luke 13:7*

A couple of years ago, we adopted a pear tree in a local community garden but we were told that we could only expect to see fruit after a few years of growth. Most fruit trees only produce fruit after three to five years. The fig tree in this parable was within this time frame and so the gardener asked for another year to help it bear fruit. Likewise the Lord gives us time to put down roots as a new believer and to become established in the faith but then there comes a time when He will look for and expect to find fruit from our lives. How do we do this? Through the power of the Holy Spirit we will be able to produce the fruit of the Spirit and bring glory to God.

## September 28

*When Jesus saw her, he called her forward and said to her, "Woman, you are set free from your infirmity." Then he put his hands on her, and immediately she straightened up and praised God. Luke 13:12*

I recently heard a minister share a vision that he had of Jesus being whipped by the Romans and being told that it was so that we could be healed, fulfilling Isaiah 53:5 that "by His stripes we are healed." He was told that the promise of healing is as certain as the promise of salvation and that we should not doubt it but believe. If you need healing today then take hold of this great and wonderful promise and receive the words of Jesus above as if He was saying it directly to you, for He is.

## September 29

Since everything will be destroyed in this way, what kind of people ought you to be? You ought to live holy and godly lives as you look forward to the day of God and speed its coming. 2 Peter 3:11-12

We know the world and universe will one day come to an end and be replaced with a new heavens and earth and we look forward to that day. If it feels like it is delayed then it is so more people can be saved. God doesn't want anyone to perish but all to repent and turn to Him and He will not come back until the fullness of time has come. We can speed His coming though through two key areas: one is through evangelism and the other is prayer. Our ministry is based on these two pillars. Make a fresh commitment today to tell others the good news and to spend time with the Lord and He will soon come.

## September 30

I tell you that in the same way there will be more rejoicing in heaven over one sinner who repents than over ninety-nine righteous persons who do not need to repent. Luke 15:17

We often think that success in evangelism is seeing hundreds and thousands come to Christ, but Jesus actually tells us that heaven celebrates when one lost soul comes into the kingdom of God. When I started reaching out with the gospel, I would lead individual people to Jesus now and again but always felt I needed to reach more. Now I realise these individuals are precious to the Lord and who knows, one of them could be the next world changer to affect multitudes. Ask God to use you to find that one lost sheep whether it's a family member, work colleague or friend today.

## October 1

*...continue in him, so that when he appears we may be confident and unashamed before Him at his coming. 1 John 2:28*

It is not how we start but how we finish that matters. Many believers have not had a great start and in fact some have lived a very godless life before coming to faith, but we are saved by grace through faith and have now become the righteousness of God in Christ Jesus. We should be always looking to grow, mature and progress in our walk with the Lord and not go backwards, stagnate or plateau. Our faith is alive and dynamic and 2 Corinthians 4:16 tells us that we are being inwardly renewed everyday. Don't stop seeking the Lord and don't give up in your battle against the enemy, for in Christ we have already won!

## October 2

*There is no fear in love. But perfect love drives out fear, because fear has to do with punishment. The one who fears is not made perfect in love. 1 John 4:18*

Fear is one of the main tactics of the enemy: fear of rejection, fear of failure, fear of attack, fear of the future. The list is endless and we can either choose to live in fear or not. The solution as always is found in God and it is to be consumed with His perfect love. We do this by abiding with Him and meditating on His word, for this is how we discover the great and awesome love that God had for us in that He gave up His only Son Jesus for us. Paul became convinced later in his life and ministry that the love of God for us is so strong that nothing in earth, heaven or hell could separate us from it. Make the choice today to receive God's love and acceptance and refuse to allow any fear to have any place in your life.

## October 3

*This is the confidence we have in approaching God: that if we ask anything according to his will, he hears us. 1 John 5:14*

God delights in both hearing our prayers and responding to them. Every good gift comes from Him and we can approach Him confidently knowing that He will not deny us what is part of His plan. How do we know what His plan and will is? Romans 12:2 says, "Do not conform to the pattern of this world, but be transformed by the renewing of your mind. Then you will be able to test and approve what God's will is—his good, pleasing and perfect will."

## October 4

*I hope to visit you and talk with you face to face, so that our joy may be complete. 2 John 1:12*

We live in an age of advanced technology more than any generation before us and it just keeps increasing at a faster and faster rate. Our phones are now more powerful than most computers and we can talk to people across the world without having to leave our home! While this is incredibly useful and convenient, it does not take away from the need to meet other believers in the flesh. There is something special about being in the presence of another person whether it's a friend or family member. The early church met daily in homes and ate and prayed together and the church multiplied and there was much joy, awe and wonder. Use technology to your advantage but also make it your aim to connect with others as much as you possibly can in real life for gadgets will disappear, but we will be with each other forever.

## October 5

*The Israelites were subdued on that occasion, and the people of Judah were victorious because they relied on the LORD, the God of their ancestors. 2 Chronicles 13:18*

What a great lesson for us in relying on God and not in our own strength or abilities. We are only victorious through the power of the Holy Spirit and not in our own might. We do not have to be clever, special or elite to call out to the Lord for help: in fact He loves to respond to the cries of His Holy Ones and come to their rescue. If you're facing a battle or obstacle today then make going to God your first priority and not your last resort and watch what He will do on your behalf.

## October 6

*But I did not believe what they said until I came and saw with my own eyes. 2 Chronicles 9:6*

When we meet the Lord face to face it will be unlike anything we have been used to on earth. When people testify about visiting heaven, they are never the same having seen things that are difficult to describe with mere human words. 1 Corinthians 2:9 says that no eye or ear has seen what God has laid up and prepared for His people but these things are revealed by the Holy Spirit for God's kingdom is not flesh and blood but spiritual. When godly people in the Bible really sought the Lord they had celestial visions of glory that now give us a glimpse of what we will experience, but even then it will be so much greater when we see it for ourselves. Let this encourage you when all you can see is the pain, problems and the brokenness of this life.

# October 7

*But you, dear friends, by building yourselves up in your most holy faith and praying in the Holy Spirit. Jude 1:20-21*

Jude talks about the kind of people who will be around in the last days just before Christ comes back and he concludes with the above advice to stay spiritually strong. I recently heard a minister share that his father had a vision of the end times and how seductive spirits would appear and try to tempt the church. The antidote to this was "to pray excessively in the Holy Spirit." One of the ways we can do this is to pray in tongues at any given moment for even when we don't know what to pray for, when we pray in tongues our spirit communicates with God in a way that bypasses our minds so that we can release what the Lord knows we need at that moment.

# October 8

*The revelation from Jesus Christ, which God gave him to show his servants what must soon take place. Revelation 1:1*

There has been more attention, discussion and debate around the book of Revelation in recent times than any other book of the Bible. This is not a bad thing since we are living in the very last days and should be watchful and aware of the times we are in, but we need to remember that the last book of the Bible is about Jesus - not the antichrist, beast system, tribulation or any other subject. He is there at the beginning and there at the end which is why He is called the Alpha and Omega and all the events that will take place very soon, are all in preparation of His great and glorious coming return. Make it the goal of your life to seek Him more than anything else in these remaining days.

## October 9

*Since you have kept my command to endure patiently, I will also keep you from the hour of trial that is going to come on the whole world to test the inhabitants of the earth.* Revelation 3:10

Jesus warned that an hour of trial would come upon the world, but not upon the true church. Bible teachers believe this is referring to the seven year tribulation period, for it will be a time of evil and distress unlike any other time in history. The church in Philadelphia were commended for holding onto their faith in the midst of trials and were promised deliverance as a result. I believe this promise is for us also who are living in the last days that we can be assured of being taken out of the final culmination of world history and be caught up in the clouds together with Jesus forever.

## October 10

*I have no greater joy than to hear that my children are walking in the truth.* 3 John 1:4

From time to time my children will surprise me by saying something profound about God or spontaneously praying about something without me telling them to. It doesn't happen all the time but when it does it brings me great joy for it reminds me that God is still at work in their lives and although they are still young and learning, my prayers and investment are not in vain. It is the same in the church for when we hear about other believers still following the Lord and serving Him despite challenges and opposition, it motivates us to keep going and not give up. Keep praying for those around you today and don't stop sharing God's love for we will eventually reap a harvest in those we have invested in.

## October 11

*One nation was being crushed by another and one city by another, because God was troubling them with every kind of distress.* 2 Chronicles 15:6-7

Although the above verses come from Old Testament times they apply for us in the days we are in. Jesus said that just before His return, nation would fight against nation and kingdom against kingdom and there would be great distress and fear on all people. In the midst of it all though the gospel would be preached to all nations and those who endured would be saved. We can be assured today that no matter what is going on in the world, we can carry out God's plans by His grace and get to the finish line for our eternal reward.

## October 12

*...grace and truth came through Jesus Christ.* John 1:17

We would be truly lost without Jesus! If He had never come into the world then mankind would still be trapped under the law. For the law came to point out sin in us and show us our fallen state, but grace came to bring us back to God and help us to become the righteousness of God. Jesus was full of grace and truth and is still pouring it out upon His people so that we can live lives that honour Him and so that we can be victorious over sin and the world. Earlier this year, I was wrestling with a challenging situation in prayer and then saw Jesus appear and say "My grace is sufficient for you for My power is made perfect in weakness." This gave me the strength to keep going and I pray that you'll receive that same grace today to keep following Him.

## October 13

*After this I looked, and there before me was a door standing open in heaven. Revelation 4:1*

In the first three chapters of Revelation, Jesus addresses the church and warns them to get ready and get right. In chapter four, Jesus calls John to ascend into heaven with a voice like a trumpet and then John is immediately before the throne and the tribulation begins shortly after. Some have interpreted this scene in Revelation as the rapture of the church for there is an ascension to heaven, with a trumpet-like voice and then the tribulation starts. Also it's interesting that the church is not mentioned again from this chapter onwards, until Jesus comes back and restores all things. Whether it represents the time of the rapture or not, it's a great reminder to be ready for that day at all times.

## October 14

*'Return to me,' declares the LORD Almighty, 'and I will return to you,' says the LORD Almighty. Zechariah 1:3*

No matter how far a person has drifted or gone away from the Lord, there is always the chance to come back and get right while we have breath in our lungs. Even if you've gone off course for one day, you can make a fresh start in the morning and seek God's presence and the Holy Spirit afresh. We serve a merciful and gracious God who does not treat us as our sins deserve but welcomes all who come to Him and the more we receive His great grace in our lives, the more we should make the commitment to never go astray again. If you hear His voice calling you to come home today then do not ignore it but quickly and humbly respond and return to His love.

## October 15

"I sent you to reap what you have not worked for." John 4:38

I'll never forget the time when God opened up a door for salvation at a local summer funfair in a town near me. I had promised to take my children there to enjoy some rides and while there felt promoted to share the gospel with those working at the fair. This resulted in a number of them praying the sinner's prayer with me and encountering God for themselves. I later found out that the father of a friend of mine had faithfully sown the gospel at that fair a number of years before, which meant I was able to go in and reap with very little effort or resistance. Remember, sometimes we sow and sometimes we reap but one day we will enjoy the harvest together.

## October 16

'And I myself will be a wall of fire around it,' declares the LORD, 'and I will be its glory within.' Zechariah 2:10

Most of Zechariah 2 is looking ahead to the millennial rule of Christ after He has returned to the earth in great power and glory, but I believe we can see glimpses of these future promises now. For God protected Nehemiah and the people as they rebuilt the walls of Jerusalem around 445 BC and God can protect us as we serve Him and build His kingdom together. In Hebrews 13:5 God promised that He would never leave us or forsake us and in Matthew 28:20 Jesus said that He would be with us till the very end of the age. So ask Him to be a wall of fire around you today and around your family, church, city and nation and that His glory would rest upon you.

## October 17

...whatever the Father does the Son also does. John 5:19

When Jesus was on the earth, He didn't go around doing just what He wanted or felt like doing, but was continually led by what He saw God the Father doing. This is why Jesus would get up early in the morning and spend time in prayer before anyone else was awake so that He knew exactly where to go and what to do for that day. If this is how Jesus operated when He was alive then how much more should we be seeking to do God's will rather than our own. Rather than pursue an idea and ask God to bless it, ask the Holy Spirit, who leads us into all truth, to show us which way to take and what to give our time to. The Spirit will show us what the Father is doing today.

## October 18

As they began to sing and praise, the LORD set ambushes against the men of Ammon and Moab and Mount Seir who were invading Judah, and they were defeated. 2 Chronicles 20:22

When king Jehoshaphat heard that a vast army was coming against Judah he famously said to God, "We do not know what to do, but our eyes are on you" (2 Chronicles 20:12) and the Lord told Him that he would be supernaturally delivered and would not have to fight this battle. He then marched out with the army with praise and singing and the enemy turned on itself and was destroyed. The people then returned back with more praise to God for His intervention. If you're facing a situation today that seems overwhelming then keep your eyes on Jesus and praise Him for the victory and watch what the Lord will do as you worship Him.

## October 19

*As long as it is day, we must do the works of Him who sent me. Night is coming, when no one can work. While I am in the world, I am the light of the world. John 9:4-5*

I am a big fan of light and in fact my name Luke means light. I would rather sleep in a bright and sunny room than a dark one. We need light to work and live and see what we are doing and where we are going. This applies in the spiritual as well and when the Holy Spirit shows us a rhema word from the Bible it is like God's light shining in our hearts revealing a hidden truth. We must keep walking in the light of God's presence and refuse to have anything to do with the darkness of this age. If we love Jesus then we will love the light for He is the Light of the world and will shine through us for all to see.

## October 20

*My sheep listen to my voice; I know them, and they follow me. I give them eternal life, and they shall never perish; no one will snatch them out of my hand. John 10:27-28*

When someone comes to faith, it is because they are responding to the prompting of the Holy Spirit and the voice of Jesus. We cannot come to Him unless we are called and we cannot repent unless there is conviction. Once we give our lives to Him, we become His sheep and His people forever and no demon in hell can snatch us away from Him no matter how much they try. Pray and remind yourself of this whenever you have a loved one that is being attacked or enticed by the enemy that they will come back to the Great Shepherd of their souls and remain with Him.

## October 21

*They triumphed over him by the blood of the Lamb and by the word of their testimony. Revelation 12:11*

We cannot escape the attacks of the devil while here on the earth but we can walk in victory over him. Even in the last days, right at the end of time, believers can triumph over the accuser of the brethren through three ways. Firstly, we need to understand the power of the blood of Jesus and apply it to every challenging situation. Secondly, we need to know the word of God and confess it in every battle that we face. Thirdly, we must do what Jesus told us to do and not try to hold onto our lives in this life, but to be willing to lose it for His Name's sake. If we can use these three weapons whenever the enemy strikes, then we will always win against him.

## October 22

*When he heard this, Jesus said, "This sickness will not end in death." John 11:4*

We do not have to accept the doctor's report as the final word over our lives, for only God knows the number of our days and He has already determined the day of our birth and death. In fact, some ministers believe that we can choose when we want to go and be with the Lord. Jesus said that we can do the impossible with the right amount of faith and if you're facing a death sentence in any area of your life then do not just accept it, but ask God for a scripture and promise to hold onto in the midst of it and refuse to let go. Jesus broke the power of sin and death for us forever so we do not have to be subject to its threats anymore, but can walk in His abundant life that He has given us instead.

# October 23

*As long as he sought the LORD, God gave him success. 2 Chronicles 26:5*

Our greatest aim and pursuit in life above everything else should be to seek the Lord. He should be our number one priority and focus and if we find we've drifted in our faith then we must come back to Him as soon as possible. Uzziah sought God while he was under the godly influence and mentorship of Zechariah but after Uzziah had increased in riches and fame, he became proud and no longer put God first leading to his downfall. Our faith and walk with Jesus will be tested when we go through difficult and trying times and it will be tested when things are going well and we feel like we have made it in life. In both cases, we must resolutely keep Him as the centre of our lives and refuse to let go.

# October 24

*…on account of him many of the Jews were going over to Jesus and believing in him. John 12:10-11*

Just as Jesus raised Lazarus from the dead leading many to put their trust in Him, so too is He raising up men and women as evangelists and heralds and prophetic voices in these last days to point people to Him. You can join this end time army simply by making yourself available for the Lord to use. You don't need to be super gifted or talented and it doesn't matter what you've done in the past, you just need to be willing to say yes to Jesus now and follow Him wherever He leads you. Some of the greatest preachers were once the greatest sinners before they were saved like the apostle Paul, but once the fire of God took hold of them, there was no stopping them!

## October 25

*Peace I leave with you; my peace I give you. I do not give to you as the world gives. Do not let your hearts be troubled and do not be afraid. John 14:27*

Jesus was about to suffer the most horrific suffering and death which would turn the lives of the disciples upside down forever and yet He told them to stay in peace and not be troubled or afraid. This same exhortation applies to us as well living in the very last days for there are many reasons to panic and fear on a daily basis but Jesus promises to be with us and keep us if we remain in Him and follow His truth. Receive His shalom peace today as you go about your day and do not let anything or anyone take it away from you.

## October 26

*This calls for patient endurance on the part of the people of God who keep his commands and remain faithful to Jesus. Revelation 14:12*

Life does not always go according to plan or run to our timetable, which is why we need to patiently wait for God to work things out in His perfect timing and way. He says in Psalm 46:10 "be still and know that I am God." The result of doing this will be a fresh infusion of grace and strength to stay in the race and keep enduring the tests and challenges that serve to make us more like Christ. I've had to wait for years and even decades for some promises to be fulfilled but I've needed to go through the process of endurance in order to develop the character I needed to handle what God wanted to give me. Keep trusting Him for there is a reward for you if you don't give up along the way.

## October 27

*On that day…I will make Jerusalem an immovable rock for all the nations. Zechariah 12:3*

There are various gatherings that take place in the Bible. Those who died in the Old Testament were said to be gathered to their people. Armies were gathered for battle and God's people were gathered together to meet with Him at different times. Israel was regathered as a nation in 1948 and even now more and more Jewish people are being gathered back to the land in fulfilment of God's word. The greatest gathering for us as Christians will be when we are gathered together in the clouds to meet the Lord in the air, which won't be long now!

## October 28

*If you remain in me and my words remain in you, ask whatever you wish, and it will be done for you. John 15:7*

If we want to have our prayers answered and bear fruit for God's kingdom then we must be willing to stay in fellowship with Christ. Too many of us drift in and out of our relationship with Him and sometimes only run back when we are in trouble. If we can walk with the Lord on a daily and consistent basis then we will be so full of His word and Spirit that His desires will become our desires and even before we call He will answer. Don't be discouraged if you've not been able to maintain this but run back to Him today and make Him your priority by setting time aside just for you to dwell in His presence.

## October 29

In everything that he undertook in the service of God's temple and in obedience to the law and the commands, he sought his God and worked wholeheartedly. And so he prospered. 2 Chronicles 31:21

How much time, energy, commitment and dedication do we give to the church and kingdom of God? Do we give as least as possible or do we go the extra mile and look for ways in which we can serve and be a blessing. The answer to this question will determine how much of God's blessing and favour will rest upon us. Hezekiah was fully committed to serving God and prospered as a result. Moses also was "faithful in all God's house" (Hebrews 3:6) and the ultimate example for us was Jesus who gave everything so that we could know God and be a part of His family. Ask the Holy Spirit to show you how you can serve and support the body of Christ today, for in helping others, you too will be helped.

## October 30

But when he, the Spirit of truth, comes, he will guide you into all the truth...and he will tell you what is yet to come. John 16:13

Too often we try to work things out and rationalise our way forward when it would be so much easier to be led by the Spirit of God. There have been a number of occasions when I've asked the Holy Spirit for an answer to a question in my mind or for help in finding a lost item and He has answered me every time. When we listen to the Holy Spirit we are listening to God and all who are led and guided by the Spirit are legitimate children of God. Don't waste time and strength trying to navigate your own way through life but look to your heavenly counsellor and guide today.

# October 31

*In his distress he sought the favor of the LORD his God and humbled himself greatly before the God of his ancestors. 2 Chronicles 33:12*

Manasseh is one of the greatest examples in the Bible of a person who was once very wicked but who then turned to God in repentance and was saved. We often look at people who are living in opposition to God's ways as lost causes or too hard to reach, but we forget that the Holy Spirit is able to turn around the most hardened sinner and bring them to faith. Just look at the transformation of Saul the persecutor of the church who became Paul the greatest ambassador for Christ. If there is someone in your life, family or workplace today that seems too far gone, don't give up praying for their salvation for they might just be the very person God wants to use and we need to remember that nothing is impossible with Him!

## November 1

> Then the angel said to me, "Write this: Blessed are those who are invited to the wedding supper of the Lamb!" And he added, "These are the true words of God." Revelation 19:9

This year saw one of the most expensive weddings ever in history and many of the guests were leaders, former prime ministers and presidents and celebrities. It's not a patch on the wedding that is to come in heaven though - the wedding between Christ and His church. This will be the most joy-filled event that we have ever encountered since first coming to faith in Jesus and will be our true "happily ever after" moment when we are joined with the Lord for all eternity. No wonder the Bible tells us to go into all the world and invite as many people as possible to this great event for there is no other place we will want to be than at that heavenly marriage of the Lamb.

## November 2

> In the eighth year of his reign, while he was still young, he began to seek the God of his father David. 2 Chronicles 34:3

There is no restriction to how old or young a person can be in seeking the Lord. Josiah sought God at the age of sixteen. This can often be a difficult age for some teenagers as it's in the transition stage between young person and adult, but nothing is impossible with prayer. If you have a loved one who is a teenager and struggling with life and faith then commit to praying for them daily to help carry them through this time of life. I was fifteen when I made up my mind that I wanted to serve the Lord for my career and this took me on a path which has led to what I'm doing now. There is still hope for our children and young people.

# November 3

*He who was seated on the throne said, "I am making everything new!" Revelation 21:5*

Sometimes things need to be changed and replaced because they are old and worn out and are no longer fit for purpose. It's always a nice feeling to buy something new - whether it's a vehicle, an item of clothing or piece of furniture - it gives us a sense of a fresh start. It gives us great hope to think that God is going to renew and change almost everything around us including the heavens and the earth and even our bodies, but even before then the Lord is able to make things new in our lives. If this is what you need today then ask Him for that new beginning in your marriage, body, work or ministry and believe that He has the power to restore, redeem and transform anything we bring before Him in prayer.

# November 4

*Again Jesus said, "Peace be with you! As the Father has sent me, I am sending you." John 20:21*

These were some of the first recorded words of Jesus to the disciples after He had risen from the dead. He did not appear and say "repent of your sins" or "why did you run away when I was arrested" but He tried to reassure them and calm their fears, before giving them a new purpose. The same response is true for many who have died and met Jesus in heaven or had an outer body experience with the Lord - He is slow to judge or condemn and quick to love and forgive. With this in mind, come and sit with Him today believing that He is ready to receive you, heal you, help you and love you. Jesus just wants to be with you.

## November 5

Look, I am coming soon! My reward is with me, and I will give to each person according to what they have done. Revelation 22:12

Christ's return for His bride is now closer than ever and when He comes to get us we will all stand before Him at the Bema seat where we will be judged as believers on what we have done for Him. Rewards and crowns will be given to those who have faithfully and diligently served the Lord and used their gifts and resources for His kingdom. This should be a reminder for us not to bury our talent in the ground but to look for ways to serve Jesus and the church in any way we can and live a life that pleases and reflects Him. We can only do this through the help and infilling of the Holy Spirit today.

## November 6

But for you who revere my name, the sun of righteousness will rise with healing in its rays. And you will go out and frolic like well-fed calves. Malachi 4:2

The Bible clearly and consistently promises healing to the people of God and here it comes through Jesus "the sun of righteousness". When He was here on the earth, He went around doing good and healing all who came to Him but it didn't stop after He ascended. Now we, the church, have been commissioned to go into all the world and preach the gospel which promises salvation and healing in His name. Come to Jesus today if you need healing or a fresh touch and invite others to receive this gift of life that He wants to give them. It's available for us all today.

## November 7

*And God said, "Let there be light," and there was light. God saw that the light was good, and he separated the light from the darkness. Genesis 1:3-4*

It was no coincidence that these were the very first words of God, for we cannot do anything without light. Light reveals, illuminates, exposes, shines, guides and by it we work, travel, socialise, interact and live our lives. John takes it even further when he says that "God is light; in him there is no darkness at all" (1 John 1:6) and that we cannot truly follow Him if we remain in the dark. This is why the enemy is associated with the darkness and night for it is the opposite to what God represents. Make every effort to stay in the light of God's presence and if you feel you're in a dark place and can't see the way forward ask the Holy Spirit to shine the light of Christ on your path in order to see which way to go.

## November 8

*She will give birth to a son, and you are to give him the name Jesus, because he will save his people from their sins. Matthew 1:21*

Jesus has many names that each reveal a different aspect of His character and role. He is called Immanuel meaning "God with us" and Alpha and Omega meaning "the first and the last" but the most important one is His Hebrew birth name Yeshua which translates into English as Jesus and means "salvation". Every person in the world needs to know Jesus as their Lord and Saviour before anything else, for we all need rescuing from sin and death. After that we can embrace the other facets of Christ's character and know Him as our healer, provider, comforter, champion and friend.

## November 9

By the seventh day God had finished the work he had been doing; so on the seventh day he rested from all his work. Genesis 2:2

In just seven days and one chapter of the Bible, God had finished creating mankind and the heavens and the earth and even set aside a day to rest at the end of it. The remainder of the Bible is all about God's restoration of man to Himself after sinning and going astray and takes over three thousand chapters to complete! I've learnt by personal experience that when we truly work with God in His way and in His timing, things get done much quicker and smoother than when we try to do things in our own strength without Him. One hour in prayer can turn a whole day around and release God's favour into our lives and situations and save us a lot of unnecessary striving and effort. So put Him first today and you'll succeed much sooner.

## November 10

On coming to the house, they saw the child with his mother Mary, and they bowed down and worshiped him. Matthew 2:11

Jesus was born in a stable but He didn't stay there. When the wise men finally found Him He was at least six months old or more and living in a home. Your beginning might be rough but it doesn't have to stay like that whether it's in a relationship, ministry, work or life. God is able to help us settle in a place that we can call home and find rest in. 1 Thessalonians 5:24 reminds us that "The one who calls you is faithful, and he will do it." So don't despise or belittle your current situation or small beginnings for it doesn't need to be where you end up and with the Lord's help you can find where you're meant to be.

## November 11

*Now the serpent was more crafty than any of the wild animals the LORD God had made. He said to the woman, "Did God really say, 'You must not eat from any tree in the garden'? " Genesis 3:1*

Some Bible teachers believe that in the beginning, Adam and Eve could communicate with certain animals in the garden and the serpent was one of them. They also believe there is good evidence that the serpent actually had legs and could stand! This would make sense in the light of God's curse upon it saying "You will crawl on your belly and you will eat dust all the days of your life." (Genesis 3:14). It also reminds us that no matter how the enemy tries to tempt us or attack us, He will always be under our feet since Jesus crushed his head at the cross as God promised He would.

## November 12

*Repent, then, and turn to God, so that your sins may be wiped out, that times of refreshing may come from the Lord, and that he may send the Messiah, who has been appointed for you—even Jesus. Acts 3:19-20*

When I read this verse, it was like I was seeing it for the very first time. It suddenly occurred to me that Jesus cannot come back until Israel collectively repents as a nation and turns back to Him. This will happen during the Great Tribulation after the Antichrist breaks his covenant with the people and takes over Jerusalem. Although two thirds of the population will be killed, a third will be saved and turn to the Lord acknowledging Jesus as the Messiah as Zechariah 13:8-9 tells us. Pray for the peace of Jerusalem today and especially that the Jewish nation would corporately repent and come to a saving knowledge of Yeshua today.

## November 13

"It is written: 'Man shall not live on bread alone, but on every word that comes from the mouth of God.'" Matthew 4:4

The Bible describes God's word like food and drink on a number of occasions highlighting the fact that we need to feed our souls as much as we feed our bodies. If we don't then our spirits will become malnourished and weak and vulnerable to the devil's attacks. One of the things we need is a direct word from God. The Greek for "word" used here is rhema and describes a direct revelation that is spoken to us by God. We can read a passage of scripture over and over but when God brings it alive and makes it applicable to our current situation then it becomes a living, active rhema word for us! Ask the Holy Spirit to give you a rhema word today and He will open the Bible to you like never before.

## November 14

This is the written account of Adam's family line. Genesis 5:1

In this chapter of the Bible we find a remez, which in Jewish understanding of scripture, is a deeper or hidden meaning behind the immediate text. When you take all the names in this genealogy and translate them using a Hebrew dictionary, you discover an incredible statement that talks about the fall and God's solution to it. In essence, it is saying that man would encounter sorrow but that God would come down to teach us and through His death, He would comfort and give us rest. Obviously it's talking about Jesus, who does give us rest and peace from all our troubles and it can surely be no coincidence that the names listed spell out this cryptic message, for names always have a significant meaning and give a clue to the destiny of that person!

# November 15

*Noah did everything just as God commanded him. Genesis 6:22*

Both Noah and Moses had a relationship with God and received specific instructions from Him about how to guide and protect the people around them. Noah built an ark at God's command and Moses built a tabernacle and both structures were designed to accommodate the mercy of God in the midst of sin and judgement. Both men were careful to build according to the pattern they had received. We've also been given divine instructions on how to escape the corruption of this world and it's found in following Jesus Christ, who only did what He saw the Father doing and was faithful to obey Him. It's also found in reading and applying the word of God which is able to save us and those around us if we continue in its truth.

# November 16

*So do not worry, saying, 'What shall we eat?' or 'What shall we drink?' or 'What shall we wear?' Matthew 6:33*

I was about to travel abroad to speak at a conference for the first time and started to worry about what clothes and items I would need for the climate and culture. After going around in circles, I decided to cast my cares on the Lord and look to the Holy Spirit to take care of everything and it eventually all worked out. He knows what we need and when we need it and has promised to provide the right food, drink and clothing as we keep our eyes on Him. Some of my best shopping experiences have been after a time of prayer and being in His presence and some of my worst experiences have been when we've rushed out and tried to do things in my own strength. So it always pays to put God first!

## November 17

> Seven days from now I will send rain on the earth for forty days and forty nights. Genesis 7:4

God told Noah exactly when He would bring judgement on the earth so that He knew when to go into the ark for safety. He has also told us through the Bible how long the tribulation period will last and what signs we can expect to see around that time. The end of the world should not be a surprise to believers for as Amos 3:7 points out, "the Sovereign LORD does nothing without revealing his plan to his servants the prophets." A lady recently shared a dream that she and others had gathered in a field to see Christ appear in the clouds and were caught up with Him and suddenly in heaven. This made me think that perhaps we will know the season as it approaches so that we can go out and meet the bridegroom as Jesus said we would!

## November 18

> Then God said to Noah, "Come out of the ark, you and your wife and your sons and their wives." Genesis 8:15-17

There are times when God calls us to come aside and walk with Him away from the busyness of life and then there are times when He releases us into a new area of service or visibility. I still remember when He told me I was coming out of the obscure and hidden workplace that I was in and true to His word, I began reaching people globally with His word on the same day. When God shuts us in, it is for our own good to dwell and learn in the secret place and when He sends us out, it is for the good of others so that we can show them what He has shown to us. Embrace both seasons for we need them both.

## November 19

*I say to you that many will come from the east and the west, and will take their places at the feast with Abraham, Isaac and Jacob in the kingdom of heaven. Matthew 8:11*

Many years ago, I was invited to the wedding of a relative and asked to rap there. I wrote a song about the coming wedding of the Lamb and the chorus went, "come to the wedding, come to the feast, come to the banquet the west and the east!" Jesus made it quite clear that there will be a great banquet in heaven and that both Jew and Gentle will sit down together and eat it. There is also a place reserved for us now that we have put our trust in Jesus and His atoning work at the cross and we will not be alone, but will be surrounded by family and friends who also followed Him during this life.


## November 20

*When he saw the crowds, he had compassion on them, because they were harassed and helpless, like sheep without a shepherd. Matthew 9:36*

People are in the same place today as they were in Jesus' day. Despite all the technological advances that we have made and the abundant materialism and resources available to us, people are still lost, unhappy and stressed. This is simply because God is not the centre of their lives. So many try to live life on their own terms, in their own strength and for their own pleasure and don't give the Lord a second thought. They fail to realise that He is the only one who can bring life, meaning, purpose and joy to their lives. In light of this, pray for those around you in the darkness and take every opportunity to share the hope of Christ with them.

## November 21

*He fell to the ground and heard a voice say to him, "Saul, Saul, why do you persecute me?" Acts 9:4*

Paul thought he was on the right path in life until Jesus appeared to him and showed him otherwise. Sometimes we busily go through life thinking that what we are doing is the right course of action, until the Lord steps in and shows us another way. This has happened to me on more than one occasion and I'm glad that God was gracious in redirecting me into His good and perfect will. He may even be speaking to you today about some decisions you need to make for the future and if it's the case then choose to follow the promptings of the Holy Spirit so that His favour and grace can continue to rest upon you.

## November 22

*Take my yoke upon you and learn from me, for I am gentle and humble in heart, and you will find rest for your souls. Matthew 11:29-30*

Most people who die and visit heaven don't want to come back to the earth. When they meet Jesus they are in total peace and don't even worry about the people they have left. This makes sense for Isaiah 6:9 describes Jesus as the "Prince of Peace." Where else can we find true and perfect contentment but in the author of salvation and the lover of our souls! Learn to meditate on Jesus and see yourself with Him with no distractions or fears and exchange your worries and cares for His calm and serenity. We have a daily choice whether to be burdened by the world or carry Christ in our hearts because we cannot do both. Choose Him today.

## November 23

*The LORD said to Abram after Lot had parted from him...All the land that you see I will give to you and your offspring forever." Genesis 13:14*

Abraham let Lot choose the best of the land rather than get into a conflict with him and afterward God ratified His promise that Abraham's descendants would inherit everything anyway. The more we are able to let go and let God, the more He is able to work and fight on our behalf. When we try to take matters into our own hands then we have to continue fighting our corner, but when we submit ourselves to God's sovereignty then He is able to defend and vindicate us in ways we never could. Trust the Lord today even if it looks like someone else is getting the better deal in the short time. God will work it out.

## November 24

*Jesus knew their thoughts and said to them, "Every kingdom divided against itself will be ruined, and every city or household divided against itself will not stand. Matthew 12:25*

I'm in America as I write this and politically it is a very divided nation right now with very little middle ground between each side. It's very name "the United States of America" tells us that it wasn't always like this and certainly it's one of the reasons why it has been the leading superpower for a long time. The only hope now is for a revival of God's Holy Spirit in the land to break the political and cultural divide and soften people's hearts towards each other. We have seen God do this in the past in both America and other nations and we pray that He will do it again here.

# November 25

> After this, the word of the LORD came to Abram in a vision:"Do not be afraid, Abram. I am your shield, your very great reward."
> Genesis 15:1

Just prior to this announcement from the Lord, Abraham had been offered a reward from the king of Sodom for rescuing the city from its enemies, but Abraham turned it down because he didn't want his reward to come from man, especially from such wicked people. God then honoured his decision and gave Abraham a promise of protection and provision directly from Himself. When we lay down material and earthly gain for a higher purpose and call, we make room for Jesus to be everything we need and more than we could ever have gained from anyone or anything else in the world. As the song says, "take the world, but give me Jesus."

# November 26

> The angel of the LORD also said to her: "You are now pregnant and you will give birth to a son. You shall name him Ishmael, for the LORD has heard of your misery. Genesis 16:11

The name Ishmael means "the God who hears" and he was a sign that the Lord had heard the cry of Hagar when she'd been mistreated and forced to wander in the desert. He also hears our prayers and requests as we lift them up to Him which is why we must not stop praying but keep pressing in until He answers us. Jesus told us to be like the widow who kept going to the unjust judge for justice until he gave her what she asked for. This is the evidence of faith: when we pray believing that He hears us and will answer us in the right way and at the right time. He knows what we need before we even ask so go ahead and ask Him today.

## November 27

*No longer will you be called Abram; your name will be Abraham, for I have made you a father of many nations. I will make you very fruitful; I will make nations of you, and kings will come from you.*
Genesis 17:5-6

The fifth letter of the Hebrew alphabet is Hey and is also the letter H which is found twice in Yahweh. Hey can represent the breath of God, grace, repentance and fruitfulness. When God put a Hey into Abraham and Sarah's names, they then became fruitful and had a son even later on in life! I knew someone else who was led to put a Hey into their name and the Lord has used them greatly since. Let God breath His ruach wind into your spirit to bring you alive and make you fruitful like never before!

## November 28

*Then one of them said, "I will surely return to you about this time next year, and Sarah your wife will have a son."* Genesis 18:10

Never underestimate what God can do in one year. It might seem a long time when you're looking for immediate answers, but there is usually a reason we have to wait. For instance, Israel couldn't possess the promised land right away but had to take it little by little over the course of a year or else the wild animals would have overtaken them. There is usually a process that we have to go through before we are ready to receive what we have been asking for and the Father knows how to prepare us. So if you're in a waiting season don't be discouraged for He is getting everything ready for what He wants to bring next.

## November 29

*And everyone who has left houses or brothers or sisters or father or mother or wife or children or fields for my sake will receive a hundred times as much and will inherit eternal life. Matthew 19:29*

My parents are missionaries and pioneers and as a result have moved home and area whenever God has led them to. It hasn't always been easy for them but they would rather obey God and go, than disobey Him for the sake of temporary comfort. It might be that you've had to move somewhere, change jobs or leave loved ones behind to pursue God's plan for your life. Jesus told us that if we really want to follow Him then we must be prepared to give up everything we possess in this life. He also reminded us though that there are rewards in both heaven and on earth when we trust Him and obey and nothing can be compared to what God has stored up for those who love Him.

## November 30

*They stood where they were and read...for a quarter of the day, and spent another quarter in confession and in worshipping the LORD their God. Nehemiah 9:3*

When Jesus taught the disciples to pray, He used the Lord's Prayer as a template, for it breaks down the main components of prayer into sections. There is worship, praise, thanksgiving, petition, repentance, forgiveness and so forth. As such, I have always tried to include these elements into my personal devotions so that I can cover everything in prayer and so that my walk with the Lord is not boring. Spending time with Jesus should be the most exciting and rewarding activity of our day, so let the Holy Spirit lead you in fresh expressions of fellowship with the Lord today.

## December 1

> When Paul placed his hands on them, the Holy Spirit came on them, and they spoke in tongues and prophesied. Acts 19:6

Have you received the Holy Spirit? The third person of the Trinity is promised to all those who put their faith in Jesus Christ and He empowers us to live a godly and fruitful life that brings glory to God. Without the Spirit, we cannot do what God has called us to do, nor can we be who He wants us to be. Seek the baptism of the Holy Spirit as soon as you can for it will bring a new dimension of grace, power and revelation in your life and faith and will enable you to live like Jesus here on the earth until He returns to bring us to Himself.

## December 2

> Now the LORD was gracious to Sarah as he had said, and the LORD did for Sarah what he had promised. Sarah became pregnant and bore a son to Abraham in his old age, at the very time God had promised him. Genesis 21:1-2

There is an appointed time for God's promises to come to pass in your life. Ever since I was young, I've had a desire to visit New York and knew that God had placed this great city on my heart. After decades of waiting and trusting in His timing, the Lord recently opened the door to travel there and fulfilled His promise to me. Don't fret over God's schedule for He knows what we need and when we are ready to receive it. I certainly wasn't in the place I am now ten years ago and I'm grateful that God waited till this year to release me to visit the US for it led to greater fruitfulness having been prepared in advance.

# December 3

*About five in the afternoon he went out and found still others standing around. He asked them, 'Why have you been standing here all day long doing nothing?' Matthew 20:6*

Right now, the church is in the last hour and there is one last call to serve the Lord before He returns. Like the landowner who employed workers from early on and even just before the end of the day, Christ is looking for willing souls to go into the world and gather the final harvest. Sadly, there are many Christians who are like the final workers to be hired, just standing around doing nothing because no one has released or commissioned them to serve in God's kingdom. If this is you then I want to let you know that Jesus has a unique plan for you today and is calling you to step up and step out in His authority and power and He will be with you every step of the way.

# December 4

*Then God said, "Take your son, your only son, whom you love—Isaac—and go to the region of Moriah. Sacrifice him there as a burnt offering on a mountain I will show you." Genesis 22:2*

In this major test, God was effectively asking Abraham if he was willing to do what He was going to do later on with Jesus. For Christ was God's one begotten Son, who was loved dearly by the Father and would be an offering and sacrifice for the sins of the world on the cross. It is also believed that the crucifixion took place in the same place as the binding of Isaac on Mount Moriah. God doesn't do anything randomly or by chance so the next time He asks you to do something, He's probably got a much bigger picture in mind than you realise so don't fear saying yes like Abraham did.

# December 5

*"'The Lord said to my Lord: "Sit at my right hand until I put your enemies under your feet."' Matthew 22:44*

There are times when we need to engage in spiritual warfare while we are under attack which might involve praying in tongues, praising, speaking to the enemy and so forth. Then there are other times when we need to be still and let God fight for us as He promised in Exodus 14:14. Being at peace in the presence of Jesus is actually one of the most powerful forms of warfare we can engage in and sometimes we need to just sit next to the Lord until we know the battle is over. Try it today rather than getting all worked up about what you're facing and be still before God as you let Him take control and fight for you.

# December 6

*For then there will be great distress, unequaled from the beginning of the world until now. Matthew 24:21*

The Bible teaches us that the tribulation will start when a seven year treaty is signed between Israel and the antichrist but that he will break this covenant halfway through and enter the Jewish temple and demand to be worshipped. When this happens it will release an even greater level of God's judgement and wrath upon the earth, which some refer to as the Great Tribulation. This is what Jesus is referring to in the verse above. I am of the strong belief that the true church of Christ will not be here to see this for it is the time of God's full wrath poured out upon the world and we are not appointed to God's wrath but to receive His mercy and salvation. Our prayer though is for Israel and unbelievers to find Jesus before this terrible time.

# December 7

> As Paul talked about righteousness, self-control and the judgement to come, Felix was afraid and said, "That's enough for now! You may leave. When I find it convenient, I will send for you." Acts 24:25

I sometimes use John 16:8 when praying for the lost - that the Holy Spirit would come and convict them about sin, righteousness and the judgement to come. We cannot convince people that they need Jesus; only the Spirit can show them that they are lost and sinful and are in need of a Saviour. Only the Holy Spirit can show people that true righteousness is found in Christ and not good works and only the Spirit can give them a revelation that one day we will all stand before the Lord and give an account of our lives. We can talk about this, but when the Lord brings it to light in a person's life then it is more likely to lead them to get right with Him resulting in a genuine conversion.

# December 8

> Isaac planted crops in that land and the same year reaped a hundredfold, because the LORD blessed him. Genesis 26:12

Despite a serious famine in the land, Isaac planted crops and reaped a bumper harvest. This is because the economy of heaven is not restricted or affected by the economy of earth. No matter what is going on in the world, God's kingdom is always full of provision and resources and if we are willing to tap into it then we can have an endless supply also. Psalm 37:19 backs this up in reassuring God's people that "in days of famine they will enjoy plenty." Don't fear what the news is saying today or in the future but believe the good report of the Lord.

## December 9

At that time the kingdom of heaven will be like ten virgins who took their lamps and went out to meet the bridegroom. Matthew 25:1

This parable is set in the context of the end times when Jesus is telling the disciples what will take place just before He comes back. I believe that we are now in these days and are on our way to meet the bridegroom. In fact, you might even say that we are in the midnight hour when the cry goes out that the bridegroom is on His way! The main point in this story though is about having enough oil to keep our lamps burning till He comes. This means maintaining a living, daily walk with the Lord and being filled with the Holy Spirit. We cannot live on an experience from the past but must seek God anew everyday and go directly to Him for new oil.

## December 10

Isaac answered Esau, "I have made him lord over you and have made all his relatives his servants, and I have sustained him with grain and new wine. So what can I possibly do for you, my son?" Genesis 27:37

We learn a couple of great lessons from this scene. The first is that our words have power and can change the course of a person's life. Proverbs 18:21 says "The tongue has the power of life and death, and those who love it will eat its fruit." So we must be careful to speak blessing over those around us rather than cursing. The second lesson is that a parent has great influence over the life and destiny of their child. Just a quick declaration over Jacob, changed the future of both of Isaac's sons. We must be very careful what we say to our children and over them for it will determine how they grow up and what path they take in life.

## December 11

Aware of this, Jesus said to them, "Why are you bothering this woman? She has done a beautiful thing to me. Matthew 26:10

When we do something for Jesus, it is never wasted. It might look foolish or worthless in the eyes of the world but not from God's perspective. When we give ourselves, our money or our time to Him, there is always a reward. It might not come right away but we can be assured that it will come in this life or in the next. This is why Jesus encouraged his followers to "store up for yourselves treasures in heaven, where moths and vermin do not destroy, and where thieves do not break in and steal" (Matthew 6:20). The next time you feel led to serve or honour the Lord in some way, don't think about the material or early cost or what others will think of you, just set your mind on pleasing Him.

## December 12

"Surely he was the Son of God!" Matthew 27:34

Jesus' crucifixion was one of the darkest events in the history of mankind. Yet at the same time, some of the very people who had participated in this came to see the truth that Christ was who He claimed to be and put their trust in Him. The same will be true in the tribulation period when people begin to see the wrath of God poured out on the earth and cataclysmic events take place. There will be those who continue to sin and rebel against God but there will be others who repent and cry out to Him for mercy even at the very end. This should motivate us to keep praying for the lost and to continue sharing the gospel whenever we can.

# December 13

*His appearance was like lightning, and his clothes were white as snow. Matthew 28:3*

Over the centuries, angels have been depicted in all sorts of ways: as babies, as women, as young children and as men. The Bible makes it quite clear though that they are neither male nor female but mighty and awesome beings who are commissioned to protect us, minister to us and serve the purposes of God. When someone encountered an angel in the Bible, they were often terrified by the visitation and some were even tempted to worship them because of the brilliance of their appearance. We need to remember that we are not alone in this world in our fight against the enemy but are protected and assisted by these servants of the Lord and just one angel has more power than a host of demonic forces.

# December 14

*But Paul shook the snake off into the fire and suffered no ill effects. Acts 25:5*

Paul was on his way to Rome and fulfilling a promise from God when suddenly he was bit by a deadly snake. Often we can be busy and focused in our walk with the Lord when suddenly the enemy will come out of nowhere and attack us without warning. It doesn't mean we are out of the will of God or have sinned, but rather that we are on the right path and the devil doesn't like it. Don't be afraid or shocked by his surprise strikes but do what Paul did and simply shake it off into the fire. There have been numerous times that I've had to rebuke, reject and cast off the enemy from my life and the good news is that when we tell him to leave, he will in Jesus' name!

## December 15

*Then God remembered Rachel; he listened to her and enabled her to conceive.* Genesis 30:22

God's ways are perfect even when they don't make sense or seem unfair. He knows what we need and when we need it and is not a second too early or too late. Rachel desperately wanted to have children but remained barren while her sister continued to give birth. If there is a barren area in your life today don't get bitter or resentful about it but surrender it to the Lord and ask Him to make you fruitful in that area and continue to trust Him in the waiting. One of the best things we can do in this situation is to praise, for Isaiah 54:1 says, "Sing, barren woman, you who never bore a child…because more are the children of the desolate woman than of her who has a husband."

## December 16

*For I am not ashamed of the gospel, because it is the power of God that brings salvation to everyone who believes.* Romans 1:16

Never be ashamed of the good news of Jesus and what He did at the cross for it is the only way to be saved and to know God. Even when we feel weak and inadequate in our witnessing, there is an inherent power in sharing the gospel which is able to convict unbelievers and lead them to Christ. Dramatic conversions have taken place in people after someone simply gave them a tract or told them that God loved them. It is not about our clever words, reasoning or persuasion, but it is the work of the Holy Spirit in showing someone that they are lost and cut off from God through sin and need a Saviour to bring them back. Ask the Lord for an opportunity to share this with someone today.

# December 17

*The king said, "Impale him on it!" So they impaled Haman on the pole he had set up for Mordecai. Esther 7:9-10*

Satan is continually plotting and scheming to hurt us and even destroy us if he could, but at the same time the Lord is fighting for us and will protect us as we keep in Him. In fact, He is able to take the very weapon that was designed to take us out and use it for our deliverance and the devil's downfall. The pit that has been dug for us will be the pit our enemies will fall into; the trap that has been set for us will be the trap our adversaries fall into. The day will come when our most fierce opposition will have to bow before Jesus and become a footstool for His feet and ours. Keep pressing forward towards this victory today and don't give up in your struggle to overcome for we will get there with Him.

# December 18

*God "will repay each person according to what they have done." Romans 2:6*

We are almost at the end of another year and you probably still have much to do as we prepare for the Christmas period. Even though you might want to take it easy and escape to a secluded retreat, you know that you have to keep going until it's all over. The same is true in our Christian walk for we daily wrestle with unseen forces of darkness and sometimes just want to get away from it all. Praise God that His unlimited grace is available to us in every season and situation and can supply to us what we need to keep going and not quit. We will get to that eternal place of rest and it will be worth the temporary struggle that we had here on the earth.

# December 19

*That same day King Xerxes gave Queen Esther the estate of Haman, the enemy of the Jews. And Mordecai came into the presence of the king. Esther 8:1*

We can not only see the defeat of our spiritual enemies but we can plunder them of their goods also. Jesus made this clear when He told the disciples to first bind up the strongman before taking all his belongings. The devil is a robber who comes to steal, kill and destroy but Proverbs 6:31 tells us that when the thief is caught, he must pay back sevenfold what he has stolen! Don't be content with just being saved and delivered from your enemies today but go into the courts of heaven in prayer and ask and believe for a sevenfold recompense for what you've gone through and what you lost. The Lord wants to release this.

# December 20

*He got up, rebuked the wind and said to the waves, "Quiet! Be still!" Then the wind died down and it was completely calm. Mark 4:9*

Storms in life are inevitable and will come when we least expect them to, but it doesn't mean we have to be overtaken by them. Jesus was sleeping peacefully on a boat when a furious squall arose and while the disciples were thinking they were about to die, He simply got up and commanded the storm to be still and it instantly obeyed. We have the same power that Christ had to command the spiritual winds and waves around us to settle down and turn into still waters. Let words of faith come out of your mouth to speak shalom peace into any situation that is troubling you today and watch the storm obey you!

## December 21

*Mordecai the Jew was second in rank to King Xerxes, preeminent among the Jews, and held in high esteem by his many fellow Jews.*
Esther 10:3

Have you ever noticed how God raised up men and women in the Bible to some of the highest positions in the land? Moses was an heir to Pharaoh, Joseph became the Prime Minister of Egypt, Daniel was promoted to the greatest place in Babylon next to the king and Esther and Mordecai reigned with King Xerxes in Persia. We must remember that God rules over the nations and is the High King of all the earth and He can appoint whoever He wants to at any time. Who does He raise up? Those with a humble and contrite heart, who do His will and seek to please Him and bless others. If you're looking for promotion in any area today then don't look to man but to God who alone can put us where we need to be.

## December 22

*When they came to Jesus, they saw the man who had been possessed...sitting there, dressed and in his right mind.* Mark 5:15

Jesus is the only way to true deliverance. We can take courses, read books, join programs and seek help which is all good, but Christ is the permanent chain-breaker! Every demonic power and entity must bow the knee before Him who holds the keys to death and hell itself. If you've tried everything possible to find freedom and are still bound then come to Jesus today and let Him set you free forever. I did this myself many years ago and have never been the same, but we have to be desperate for change and willing to let the master surgeon perform His divine surgery on our hearts and souls. Let Him transform your life for His glory today.

## December 23

*"Come with me by yourselves to a quiet place and get some rest."*
Mark 6:31

December can often be one of the busiest times of the year especially in the run up to Christmas and all the preparation that goes into it. We can get so busy that we forget what really matters and then wonder why we have lost our peace. In every season, we can either do things in our own strength or with God. When we continue to put the Lord first and rely on His power and Holy Spirit in every situation, we will find that we can keep going and walk in divine grace despite the pressures around us. So if you're feeling tired or run down today, come away and sit with Jesus again until you receive His anointing that never runs dry.

## December 24

*Joseph had a dream, and when he told it to his brothers, they hated him all the more. Genesis 37:5*

Be careful who you share your dreams with for not everyone will appreciate what God has put inside of you. I learnt this lesson early on like Joseph and it taught me to hold ideas and plans in my heart until the right time. Despite all the supernatural and miraculous events surrounding the birth of Jesus, Luke 2:19 says that "Mary treasured up all these things and pondered them in her heart." There are some things that I know the Lord has given me to share with the body of Christ to encourage and help them and there are other things that although wonderful and amazing are not to be released until God says so. Sometimes we have to wait until those around us are ready to receive what we have seen so that our vision can be appreciated and accepted as God intended.

# December 25

"From this day on I will bless you." Haggai 2:19

God said that He would bless the nation of Israel on the 24th day of the 9th month on the Hebrew calendar. The Jewish calendar is different to our Gregorian one so I looked up the corresponding date for the above event in the year of writing this and I was shocked to discover that it fell on Christmas Day. This was amazing because I had already had a sense that Christmas was going to be blessed in this same year and would mark the beginning of a new and better season. This same promise is always available for God's people though through Jesus for He came to give us life in abundance if we would only believe.

# December 26

But when he drew back his hand, his brother came out, and she said, "So this is how you have broken out!" And he was named Perez. Genesis 38:29

Judah refused to give his last son to his widowed daughter-in-law and instead, unknowingly got her pregnant himself. Yet despite all this complicated and messy backdrop, Perez, which means breakthrough, is later named in the gospels as one of the ancestors of Jesus Christ! This is a perfect example of God's grace operating in our lives despite our sin and failures and it also shows us that God can use us despite our past and that we can breakthrough into His promises and redemptive plans. Don't let your upbringing or anything else, stop you from taking hold of all that Christ has in store for you today.

# December 27

*The people ate and were satisfied. Afterward the disciples picked up seven basketfuls of broken pieces that were left over. Mark 8:8*

The disciples gave Jesus seven loaves and He blessed them, broke them and multiplied them to feed four thousand people. There were also seven baskets of leftovers for the disciples to take away. This is a prime illustration of how God can use whatever we give Him and multiply it many times over. We often feel that we will lose out and be in deficit if we give money or resources away, but the opposite is true, for we can never out-give God and the Bible clearly states that we will reap what we sow. If you feel led to give a gift today to bless someone or sow into a ministry for the kingdom, don't be afraid, for your gift will bless many and come back to you pressed down, shaken together and running over!

# December 28

*Therefore, there is now no condemnation for those who are in Christ Jesus. Romans 8:1*

As we prepare to go into another year, refuse to walk in condemnation, fear or shame. These three things are not from God and instead are used as weapons against us by the enemy to paralyse and immobilise us from going forward. If we have sinned then the Holy Spirit will convict us and lead us into repentance but He will never condemn us and it's important to know the difference. One is grace-based and the other is fear-based. If we continue to try and walk close to the Lord and in the Spirit then we will live above these tactics of the evil one and will instead remain in the love of the Father which casts out all fear forever.

# December 29

*...neither height nor depth, nor anything else in all creation, will be able to separate us from the love of God that is in Christ Jesus our Lord. Romans 8:39*

If the book of Romans is, as one theologian described it, "The cathedral of the Christian faith" then the verse above has to be the highest pinnacle of the building. For after laying out the naturally base and sinful condition of mankind in the preceding chapters, Paul then gives the reader great hope in the finished work of Jesus and concludes that once we've decided to live for Him in this new way of life then there is nothing that exists that can take us away from Christ's love and salvation. Hold onto this truth and promise today as we come to the end of another year and don't let the enemy tell you otherwise.

# December 30

*For the Lord will carry out his sentence on earth with speed and finality. Romans 9:28*

We are now at the stage where Bible prophecy is coming to pass and being fulfilled at an unprecedented rate. All that we are seeing in the world today was warned about by Jesus and others and is happening quickly. We are in the very end times and events are now accelerating such as the conflict in Israel and increased lawlessness. Christ Himself said, "If those days had not been cut short, no one would survive, but for the sake of the elect those days will be shortened" (Matthew 24:22). The Lord is wrapping everything up now which should cause us to give our all to Him in holiness and say "Maranatha - come quickly!"

# December 31

*Brothers and sisters, my heart's desire and prayer to God for the Israelites is that they may be saved. Romans 10:1*

One of the last miraculous events that will take place before Jesus returns is the turning of the Jewish people back to Yeshua. We know this because the Bible tells us that the nation will go through the fire but a remnant will be saved. Two thirds will perish in the tribulation but a third will come through it and give glory to God. As adopted spiritual Israelites, our mission is to pray now for the salvation of the chosen people of God. All that is happening in Israel and the Middle East is pointing towards this glorious time when the eyes of the people will be opened to see Jesus and they will fully embrace Him as Lord so that He can take His rightful place in Jerusalem as King of Kings forever, amen!

Before you go…

Can I ask you one very important question: "Do you know Jesus?" If the answer is no then I would like to introduce you to Him. He is the Son of God and the Saviour of the world and He died on a cross for your sins 2000 years ago. He didn't come to judge us, but to save us through his death and resurrection.

Romans 10:13 says "Everyone who calls on the name of the Lord will be saved." I called to Jesus at the age of 5 and asked Him to forgive me of my sins, to make me clean and to live inside of me and that is exactly what He has done for almost 40 years.

If you do not have a relationship with Jesus then invite Him into your life today and start with this prayer:

Dear Jesus,

I admit that I am a sinner and need saving. I believe that only you can save me through your death and resurrection. I repent of my sins and turn away from them today. Please come into my heart and make me clean. Show me the path that you have for me and help me to walk on it with you for the rest of my life. I can only do this through the power of the Holy Spirit.

In your name,

Amen.

If you prayed that prayer then please get in touch with us and let us know as we would love to hear from you and celebrate your new journey in Christ. Go to citylights.org.uk to send us a message.

Printed in Great Britain
by Amazon